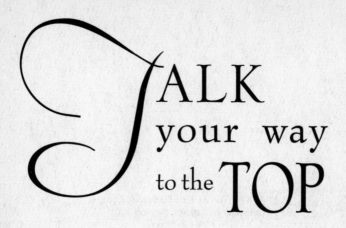

TALK your way to the TOP

TINA SANTI FLAHERTY

A PERIGEE BOOK

A Perigee Book
Published by The Berkley Publishing Group
A member of Penguin Putnam Inc.
375 Hudson Street,
New York, New York 10014

Copyright © 1999 by Tina Santi Flaherty
Cover design by Miguel Santana
Cover photo by Tom Palumbo

First edition: January 1999

Published simultaneously in Canada.

The Penguin Putnam Inc. World Wide Web site address is
http://www.penguinputnam.com

Library of Congress Cataloging-in-Publication Data

Flaherty, Tina Santi.
Talk your way to the top / Tina Santi Flaherty.
p.   cm.
ISBN 0-399-52470-3
1. Success in business.   2. Communication—Social aspects.
3. Public speaking.   I. Title.
HF5386.F4158   1999
650.1—dc21   98-39110
CIP

Printed in the United States of America

10 9 8 7 6 5 4 3 2 1

*To my mother and father, Dale Laverne Pendergrast and
Clement Alexander Santi, and my everloving grannie,
Vattie Velma Headrick, who always believed in me*

ACKNOWLEDGMENTS

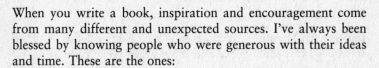

When you write a book, inspiration and encouragement come from many different and unexpected sources. I've always been blessed by knowing people who were generous with their ideas and time. These are the ones:

William E. Flaherty—My supersmart, superverbal husband who long ago talked his way into my heart. His support while I was writing this book, as well as during the previous one, never failed to amaze me.

Connie Meehan—Who cared about this book as much as she does about her pussycats, Clementina and Tosca (well, maybe!) As my in-house editor, she willingly left them day after day until everything was letter-perfect. She is an irrepressible and irreplaceable friend.

Duane Garrison Elliot—A colleague and friend, whose special savvy helped make this book better.

Patricia Francy—An insightful businesswoman and friend, who's always willing to share her ideas and experiences no matter how busy she is.

Brenda O'Hanlon—A new friend, author, and top journalist in Ireland, whose long-distance interest resulted in several hilarious anecdotes in my book, as well as in my life.

Cathy Cash—A bestselling author and pal, whose funny stories and unique experiences helped perk up this book.

Ralph Nichols—A supercommunicator who went out of his way to give me fresh insights into the power of public speaking.

Patti Printz—A long-time, supersmart friend, who's always been there when I needed her, especially if a chapter (or I) seemed to be falling apart.

Pat Nation—A noted newspaperwoman, whose super sense of humor, terrific insights and genuine interest in the book were so vey helpful.

Bill Powell—A colleague at Colgate-Palmolive, who's been my good friend ever since, and whose wise counsel was invaluable in writing this book.

Dolores McMullan—A genuinely nice person and the editor of this book. Her intelligence and input grace every page.

Don Softness—A wonderful writer and friend, who pulls no punches or legs—unless he can get away with it.

Kay Wight—A special friend and business associate, whose wit and wellspring of experiences are reflected in this book.

P.S.—Special hugs and tummy-rubs to Liam, Ashleen, and Shadow Flaherty, our beyond-beloved fur-persons, who kept me company as I wrote this book, especially in the wee, small hours of the morning.

And thanks to all the following, who in one way or another made my job easier:

Letitia Baldridge   Dale Leon Miller
Martha David   Marty Nussbaum
John Duff   Vicki and Dr. Stuart Quan
Ena Francis   Kate Roberts
Christina and Brian Flaherty   June and Tim Rooney
Peggy Lucchesi Geiser   John Rosenwald
Constance Giamo   Lew Rudin
Maria Headley   David Seiniger
Barbara Krupa   Vicky Shepherd
Regina Leon   Mimi Strong
Trip Leon   Erin Stryker
Felice Lippert   Roula Stephanides
Marina Maher   Diane Terman
Reuben Mark   Nina West

CONTENTS

Introduction

- Do you want to run away and hide whenever you have to speak in public?

- Do you find it difficult to make your point?

- Do you feel awkward mixing and mingling at company events?

- Are you never the one asked to make a presentation to a new client?

- Do you feel your boss fails to appreciate your particular talents?

- Do you use words that suggest you're not sure of yourself?

- When you talk on the phone, do people sometimes respond negatively?

- Do you wish your clothing made you look more successful?

- Are you unsure of what proper etiquette is?

If you've answered *yes* to any of the above, this book can help you get rid of some bad habits that may be holding you back.

What if I told you there's a secret weapon that men have been using forever to push themselves ahead of the pack and that this magic formula helps them jump-start their careers quicker than a speeding bullet? If you want to get on a fast track to the top, you need to know how to communicate effectively—in both spoken *and* unspoken ways.

Men have always known that the ability to pitch their ideas persuasively—whether it's behind the podium, around the conference table, or during a casual one-on-one—is an invaluable tool that wins hands down in the game of business. Men are equally tuned-in to the fact that the unspoken language of behavior, clothing, manners, and social skills also speaks volumes about their ability to reach the top.

Effective communications, whether silent or spoken, are some of the most important skills that a businesswoman can develop. It can determine whether you'll be a major success or get stuck in the middle of the pack. In her book, *Talking to Win*, Dr. Lillian Glass writes, "The image you project in your speech can determine whether a person will become your friend, lover, business associate, employer, or employee." Pure and simple, your talking image affects your whole life.

If this is true, why aren't more women aware of it? Why aren't they working night and day trying to improve their verbal image? Why aren't they begging for the opportunity to give a speech or make the big presentation to a new client? Besides pure terror and the fear of failure, I have another theory. Some women assume they won't be good at it, so they don't even try. They think that public speaking is more of a "guy thing." Women have been programmed to believe that men are the better communicators—more capable, more authoritative, with voices easier to hear and listen to. This is definitely not the case. Speaking on your feet—whether to two people or two hundred—is an equal opportunity activity.

Once equipped with the know-how, women can be just as effective as men, whether they're making a presentation in a crowded hall, schmoozing with a group, or working a room at a noisy cocktail party. The real kicker is—no one expects a woman to be that good at it. And when she is, people give her *triple* points, because their expectations were so low.

If you're given the chance to speak before a group or asked to make a presentation, grab it and run. You're being offered a one-of-a-kind opportunity to strut your stuff. Here's your chance to show you've got what it takes to be a leader. With the spotlight on *you*, and no one else, it's within your grasp to impress, persuade, sell, entertain, and, ultimately, put your career on a fast track to the top.

A seldom-acknowledged fact is that when a woman is able to master the art of effective communication, she not only surprises and amazes, but ultimately conquers. *Talk Your Way to the Top* is designed to help a woman succeed in an area that can forever change her life—on and off the job. Once women discover how much power there is in the art of communication, they'll be breaking down the doors for the chance to stand up and be heard.

I started out as a radio disc jockey, went on to become a

TV co-host, and then parlayed that talent into a business career that culminated in being elected the first female corporate vice president of the giant Colgate-Palmolive Company. It wasn't an easy task for a young, unsophisticated Southern girl, especially at a time when most women hadn't even heard of the glass ceiling, much less learned how to crack it. So how did I reach that level? I learned early on that the ability to talk and think on your feet is an invaluable asset that sets you apart from the crowd. I also learned that the way I dressed, schmoozed with my colleagues, entertained clients, wrote a memo, behaved in public, and dealt with my boss and staff, all painted a picture of my abilities as an executive.

MAKING AN IMPRESSION

Someone very wise once commented, "You don't get a second chance to make a first impression." It takes a lot of hard work to make a favorable one. Research shows that people size you up in the first five to seven seconds after they've met you. That's a tiny time frame within which to sell yourself, especially when it counts. It's estimated that in business you'll spend more than 50 percent of your time "selling"—whether it's to get a job, a raise, a budget okayed, or the go-ahead to run with a new project. And there'll always be someone who isn't buying what you're selling. Learning how to make the right impression is a complicated business. How you present your ideas and move your body sends a message, just as the way you mix and mingle at a cocktail party says something about you.

It's no wonder that trial lawyers spend countless hours making sure their clients dress, speak, and behave in an appropriate manner. Attorneys have always known that juries can be swayed—either favorably or negatively—by the way a client talks, acts, and looks. Countless defendants are seriously spruced-up and given a quick course in manners and polite-speak for their all-important court appearances.

YOU'RE ON TRIAL DAILY

If behavior, choice of clothing, and speech mannerisms can influence a jury's judgment, it's not much of a stretch to figure out that visual and verbal communications are major factors in every walk of life. In effect, *all* of us are "on trial" on a daily basis. People automatically make judgments about your professionalism and abilities based on the way you *look, speak*, and *act*. These three characteristics form the foundation of your communications ability.

• The first thing people notice is how you *look*. Since clothing, hair, and makeup speak their own language, they must be compatible with the image of a successful executive. If not, they can cancel out what you say and do. Chapter 1, *"Packaging Yourself,"* gives you a good rundown on your appearance and how to dress.

• Second, the way you *act* is just as important as how you look and talk. You've heard the old saying that actions speak louder than words. Believe it! You could look like Ms. Executive of the Year and dazzle them with words, but if you don't follow through in an executive manner, you've lost the game. What do I mean by "executive manner"? Everything from the way you interact with your boss and colleagues, to the way you handle business/social functions, to how you approach others in one-on-one situations. Chapter 4, *"Talk Like a Man, Think Like a Woman"* deals specifically with managerial style and behavior.

• The way you *speak*, the third part of the equation, is powerful medicine. You might have the greatest idea in the world, but if you flub up when you pitch it, you're finished before you start. Although most people can learn to improve the way they speak, it takes real effort. It's easy to speak and yet not communicate. You don't want to just talk *at* people, you want to talk *with* them. Good communications is a skill. And, like most other skills, it's learnable. Chapter 2, *"Maxing Your Meetings,"* and Chapter 7, *"Showtime! Giving a Speech,"* will help you learn to sell your ideas to others.

This book is designed to teach you how to communicate positively *whenever* you're on view. The rules and guidelines for effective communications aren't all that difficult. They're similar to good table manners—once learned, they become second nature. You, too, can talk your way to the top if you follow the advice in this book and put it into practice every chance you get. It's more important just to do it than to try to do it perfectly.

I recently read a comment by Andy Patti, former president

of Dial Corporation, who summed up today's job market in a single sentence: "Employers are now saying to employees, 'I make you no promises, but if you're worth more than you cost, I'll keep you around.'"

That's what this book will help *you* do—make yourself indispensable to your employer. Despite downsizing and the difficulty of making it in what is still predominantly a man's world, women who communicate effectively not only stay off the unemployment line, they continue to climb in their present jobs or get even better ones.

PACKAGING YOURSELF

"I was eight years into my career before anyone was brave enough to tell me that my clothing was holding me back. My attitude was to wear whatever appealed to me. If my mirror told me I looked good, that was enough for me. I was one of those people who thought if you messed with the way I dressed, you'd soon start messing with my head. Little did I realize that my way wasn't necessarily right."

The above is my own sad story. When I first joined Colgate-Palmolive, I dressed the way I had when I worked at Grey Advertising. Why not? After all, I'd been super-successful at the agency, winding up as its first female vice-president at the age of twenty-eight. It didn't dawn on me that these companies were two separate worlds, with distinct cultures. People dressed, spoke, and acted differently at each company. Advertising, for the most part, is casual, more individualistic, and very trendy. Corporations are usually just the opposite—staid, conservative, and trend-resistant.

COMPLETELY OUT OF IT

Oblivious to these simple facts, I fell in love with the "ethnic" look, the fashion fad then current. There I was, in the hallowed halls of Colgate-Palmolive, wearing beads, bangles, boleros with little tiny mirrors pasted all over them, big dirndl skirts, and lace-up boots. (How I could have thought I was appropriately dressed beats me!)

I clung to my "advertising" wardrobe until one unforgettable day when my boss asked to speak to me privately. He'd just returned from lunch, after one martini too many—which apparently gave him the courage to tell me something that had been bugging him for months. "Tina," he said, slurring his words, "Why do you dress like you're going to a Russian folk dance? Haven't you noticed no one else here dresses that way?" I was embarrassed and insulted, especially since I didn't think he was much of a fashion plate himself. But several days later I remembered that old bit of wisdom, _in vino veritas_—in wine there is truth—and I decided that maybe what my boss had said made sense after all. To be candid, I was clueless, and I hadn't bothered to notice how other executives in the company dressed.

I went on the biggest shopping spree of my life. I bought several inexpensive suits: some in dark, neutral shades for winter, and others in slightly paler hues for summer. To give me different looks, I bought blouses in bright colors and patterns. Since silk ones were too expensive for my budget, I settled for a fairly good brand of polyester.

Soon after I started sporting my new wardrobe, interesting things began to happen. I'm not exaggerating when I say that almost overnight I was invited to more top-level meetings than ever before, and also received a flurry of phone calls from senior management. At conferences, people started asking me for my opinion, where previously I'd had to fight to be heard. Believe me when I say that as soon as I began to look like an executive, people started treating me like one. In turn, it boosted my self-confidence, and that was just what I needed to move into the fast lane.

APPEARANCE COUNTS

All right, already—so you think you've heard everything there is to know about dressing for success. Can there possibly be anything new to add to the subject? You bet! So listen up and let it all sink in.

Believe it or not, your appearance accounts for more than half the impression you make on others. One study has shown that 55 percent of the perception people have of you is based purely on the way you look, which also includes your body language.

People size you up approximately five to seven seconds after meeting you, before you've said a single word. Based on your physical appearance, instant assumptions are made about your social status, how much money you make, how educated you are. In the final analysis, it's frequently your appearance that tells people whether or not they want to continue their association with you. Clothing, hair, and makeup reveal as much about you, if not more, than your résumé does. If packaging can motivate you to buy one lipstick over another, or choose a Ford Mustang over a Mazda Miata, why shouldn't the same standard be applied to you?

DEVELOPING AN EXECUTIVE IMAGE

Most personnel managers concur that job candidates need not only the necessary skills to get hired, but the image to match. If your appearance isn't up to par in an interview, the likelihood is your services won't be needed.

An executive image is not only necessary to get on board, it's mandatory for keeping your job and moving up. A so-so appearance makes switching to the express lane an almost impossible task. Today's competitive workplace has a low tolerance for women—and men—who look as if they don't belong. Companies can find plenty of gonnabe executives who dress as if they'd fit right in. Why sabotage your chances for real success by neglecting something that's so easy to fix, once you know how? Learning how to project an executive image, however, is entirely in *your* hands. While some people are born knowing how to dress, others, like me, have to be nudged. Whatever it takes for you to get it, just remember it's all up to you.

DRESS TO FIT THE COMPANY

How you dress depends a great deal on where you work. At an entertainment magazine, for example, it may be okay to wear leather pants and a blazer to work (unless you're meeting one of your advertisers). That's definitely not the case, however, in corporate America. In that environment, suits, dresses, and the occasional pants suit are the only way to go. Turning your image around is not brain surgery. It's merely a matter of adapting to your environment. Like a chameleon, you want to blend in—not stick out like a sore thumb.

If you aim to make it big in business, going against a company's culture and its standards of dress is a major, major mistake. Learning how to develop an executive image requires that you keep your eyes and ears wide open. Look around and observe what successful women in your company are wearing. Then check your clothing against it. Buy magazines that offer advice on executive style and scrutinize your wardrobe piece by piece. What vibes do your clothes send out? Do they say "I got up late this morning and just threw something on"? If so, you're sending a message that your job isn't that important to you. If you slap on really casual clothes—beat-up khakis, an unpressed blouse, sloppy shoes—you're signaling that you're dressed for play, not for work, and that you're not very serious about your job.

If you work for a company that permits, or even encourages, "casual Fridays," go easy. Let's face it, a man can come to work without a tie, wearing sneakers and jeans and still be viewed as an authority figure. When a woman does it, her executive status seems to vanish. She just looks like one of the "girls" in the office. A casual dress or pants and a jacket or blouse are fine, as long as they're tasteful.

No Threadbare Threads

Keep your clothes in impeccable working order. I knew a woman at one of my former companies who actually put safety pins in her dresses because she'd gotten too large for them. If your clothes are too tight, either throw them away, donate them to charity, or put them aside for a skinnier day. Whatever you do, don't wear them to work. Ditto for a crumpled suit or dress. It makes you seem crumpled yourself. Rundown heels and scuff marks on your shoes give the same impression.

It's a good rule of thumb to *always* dress as if you're planning to meet your boss for a salary review. The morning you show up in your grungiest garb could be the day you're asked to take an important client to lunch or attend an unexpected meeting with top company execs. Your appearance must be at the ready every single day of your working life. *There are no exceptions to this rule.*

Avoid Gender Confusion

Act and dress the part of a conventional woman. Extremes threaten men, who, more often then not, are the bosses. It's not necessary for a woman to dress in mannish suits or wear a guy-style haircut to be taken seriously. On the other hand, wearing short-short skirts, small sweaters, and big hair obviously detract from your business persona as well. You should aim to come off first as a professional and second as a woman.

THINK SMALL

The jewelry you wear to work shouldn't be too obvious. For example, if you want to wear earrings, avoid dangling ones. Choose small pearl or "gold" studs instead. Forget about statement necklaces. They're out of place in an office. Bracelets are also one accessory too many; a tasteful watch and one ring (not two) are all you need. Wearing big, gaudy jewelry to the office doesn't merely detract from your executive image, it kills it.

BUSINESS-STYLE SHOES AND STOCKINGS

When it comes to shoes and handbags, always make sure they at least look like leather (more tasteful), and are in matching colors. Neglecting to coordinate them can ruin your entire appearance. Choose neutral colors (beige, black, navy) and avoid overly bright shades (red, hot pink, cobalt blue, etc.). Simple closed-toe pumps are the only shoes you should be wearing to the office. Forget about sandals, running shoes, or anything clunky and complicated. Despite what television and movies would have you believe, stiletto heels are obviously not for business either. Wear low to medium heels that allow you to move freely without breaking your neck. If you ever walk down the hall with a group of guys who have to slow up because your high heels force you to move at a snail's pace, you soon realize how inappropriate these shoes are in a professional setting.

Make sure your pantyhose or stockings are either flesh-colored or black, depending on what you're wearing. Don't be caught dead in patterned stockings or any flashy colors. I once worked with a young woman who insisted on matching the color of her stockings to her dress. When she wore red, her stockings made her legs look like she had a bad rash. Also, don't wear dark stockings with light-colored clothing or shoes—you'll look like a hick from the sticks who doesn't know any better. By now, you should also know never to wear pantyhose that have a run in them. Always keep an extra pair or two in your desk in case one crops up during the course of the day.

HANDBAGS

If you frequently attend outside meetings and carry an at-taché case, a shoulder-strap purse is best, since it leaves one hand free. Make sure it's in a solid color and on the small side. It shouldn't look like a piece of luggage! One other tip— don't carry your handbag everywhere you go in the office. It broadcasts to everyone, "I'm a woman," instead of letting you blend in. Lock it in your desk drawer instead. Some successful women, particularly high-level political leaders, avoid hand-bags altogether. My friend Kay Wight, ex–vice-president of CBS and a former Commissioner on the Status of Women, deliberately chooses suits with pockets that are big enough for her makeup and change purse, so she doesn't have to carry one. And Mary Robinson, the ex-president of Ireland, was never seen with a handbag from the day she declared her candidacy to the day she left office.

GROOMING 101

Egads, grooming sounds like such a dull subject! It may be, but if you fail it you'll flunk Executive Image 101. You've probably heard most of this before, but in the interest of communicating cleanliness, here it is again.

Splish, splash—take a daily bath or shower. Some people don't, you know, and their poor co-workers suffer the results. Bad body odor is one of the most offensive things there is. There's nothing worse than standing next to a person who makes you want to hold your nose until she leaves.

Believe it, there are people who ignore the basics of cleanliness. I once supervised an otherwise lovely woman who smelled so bad that her co-workers complained to me that they didn't want to work with her anymore. Because she was a valuable employee and I liked her, I decided to talk to her about it. It was a touchy subject, of course, and although in our conversation she insisted she bathed daily (she didn't), she eventually took heed and the problem went away. The moral of this story is to bathe every day, use deodorant, and try to smell nice and clean. There's no scent any better than your own.

Excessive perfume is also a turn-off, especially to men. You can bet you've used too much if it announces your arrival before you walk through the door. I worked with an older woman at Colgate who was oblivious to this. She doused perfume on so heavily you could smell her coming around the corner. People would open their office windows after she left and fan themselves. Needless to say, her co-workers were so distracted by her perfume they found it difficult to take her ideas seriously.

Your Hands

People notice your hands more than you realize, so don't fail to keep your fingernails clean. Dirt under your nails makes people think you're dirty all over. Chipped nail polish looks just as bad as a stain on your clothes. It's also a good idea to keep your nails short. Two-inch-long Dragon Lady fingernails, whether real or fake, are totally out of place. Ditto for weird-colored polish and sequins on your nails. Avoid bright red polish. Choose a very pale pink or flesh-toned color instead. It not only looks more natural but if it chips, it's less noticeable.

Good Hair Days

Keep your hair clean and combed. The messy look doesn't belong in an office. It makes you look like an unmade bed and communicates a very non-executive image. If you color it, be savvy enough not to go too long between touch-ups. One of my clients, the president of a very large university, continually complained about his female colleagues' lack of attention to their hair coloring. It seems they would let their dark roots peek through for months on end. Because of this, he was hesitant to ask them to represent the university at important fund-raisers. It apparently didn't dawn on any of these women that just a simple bottle of hair dye was all that

stood between them and a more positive image in their boss's
eyes.

YOUR TEETH

It's amazing how some people overlook something as obvious as their teeth. Nothing ruins your good appearance faster than teeth that are yellow, crooked, or have very
noticeable gaps. To get your pearly whites in good shape, take
advantage of the new aesthetic dentistry techniques. Everything from bleaching, bonding and straightening crooked
teeth are all within your grasp. Sure, it can cost a small bun-
dle, but it can work major miracles for your appearance and
reputation. When you open your mouth, what's important is
not just what you say, but how you look when you say it.

I once had a twenty-something assistant who was quite
beautiful—until she smiled. Her teeth had a huge gap that
was in startling contrast to her cool, blond, elegant looks.
When we were chatting one day, I couldn't help but ask her—
as gently as possible—if she had ever considered fixing her
teeth. She replied that she didn't think it was necessary, which
knocked me for a loop since the space was so prominent. As
far as she was concerned, her teeth worked just fine so why
should she bother going through a lot of dental work, even
though her parents were willing to pay for it? Little did she
know that most people in the office described her as "the
pretty blonde with the great big gap in her front teeth." This
obvious flaw made her look almost goofy and killed her oth-

erwise attractive, professional appearance. Ultimately, it held her back because it was so noticeable.

BLOW ME DOWN

Pay attention to how your breath smells. Always carry breath spray, TicTacs or whatever other fresheners are on the market, to make sure your breath doesn't knock anyone over. I once worked with a top cosmetics executive who was always elegantly dressed and made-up. Everyone jokingly referred to her, however, as "old fish-breath." In spite of her liberal use of perfume, her breath was the only scent that prevailed. True, it didn't get her fired (she was too high up), but people weren't anxious to chat her up, much less sit next to her at dinner. Bad breath killed the very image she tried so hard to cultivate.

FLAB ATTACK

I'm not telling you anything you don't already know, but nothing ruins your appearance faster than flab. An over-abundance of it is not only unattractive but makes it difficult to find clothing that hangs right. When you're trim and fit, your self-confidence is high and your image is positive. Staying in shape communicates the message that you're in control of your mind and body.

BODY LANGUAGE

Your body language is an extension of your appearance. A recent article in the *Wall Street Journal* says, "Body lan-

guage . . . often is more meaningful than the spoken word."
Negative body language can be disastrous to your career, no
matter how well you manage to do everything else. Do you
move like an executive? Do your eyes project self-confidence?
Does your body send signals that show you're a winner? In
business, and in private, your body language is an important
part of your success or failure.

THE LOOK OF A LEADER

Some people have "it," others don't. Exactly what is that
complex combination that labels someone as a high-octane
executive, regardless of age or position? One important factor
in the equation is positive body language. It distinguishes winners from losers in subtle but unmistakable ways. Did you
ever see a West Point cadet who hunched over? Hardly.
There's a message there. Leaders know how to telegraph their
status by using their bodies properly. You can, too. Here's
how:

Stand tall. Keep your head high, shoulders erect, and eyes
up. All of this makes you look more confident.

Make eye contact. A real leader doesn't shy away from
connecting with people one-on-one. Make sure you maintain
direct eye contact throughout a conversation. It shows character and confidence.

Sit up straight. Leaders look interested and involved. They
sit erect and still at meetings. You should too. Don't slouch

back in your chair; you'll look bored. Instead, put your arms on the table (if there is one) and lean forward. You'll appear more involved. Don't fidget. You want to look relaxed.

Give people breathing room. Successful people realize the importance of physical space and respect the spatial requirements of others. They never stand so close that they make people feel boxed in and threatened.

Look alive. A fast-track executive knows that projecting energy and enthusiasm is vital to her or his career. Always look wide awake and ready for business, even if you were up all night. People who move slowly and look half asleep are turn-offs.

Shake hands. The most self-confident women around project it in their handshake—firm, not wimpy. They never hesitate to be the first to extend their hand. Men have always known that a friendly handshake sends out positive vibes. Some women think it's unfeminine to shake hands; they're wrong. It's an accepted and welcome business greeting.

Keep calm. Leaders know how to stay calm in a crisis, as well as in everyday life. People who are hyper about everything, who overreact to the slightest problem, rarely get ahead. Not only do they give everyone else the jitters, they can't be counted on to take charge in case of real trouble. To appear in control, avoid wringing your hands, glancing nervously around the room, or constantly wrinkling your forehead.

Show openness. Respected executives know the value of appearing open and approachable. Men especially show it by keeping their arms and feet open—not crossed—and by opening their suit jacket once they get down to business.

SMILE POWER

Want to light up your face? A whole room? Then smile! An irresistible smile makes people want to get to know you. The presence or absence of a smile carries great significance. It can communicate either personality and confidence or lack of both. Plus, a smile is a universal symbol of approval, no matter what the culture. Think of it as global chemistry.

NONVERBAL SCREW-UPS

Body language often betrays people in the workplace more than they realize. My friend, Brandi, a thirty-something stockbroker, can't seem to make the big leap forward. I often wondered why, until we were in a meeting together. I quickly realized her body language was doing her in. When she was asked a question, she looked down instead of up. All through the meeting she tapped her foot, demonstrating her nervousness. Another business associate, Brad, has a similar career problem. In one-on-one conversations, he's an articulate speaker. When he's in front of a group, however, his body starts to sway back and forth. Although Brad was not aware of this until I pointed it out, he often wondered why his audience seemed disinterested in what he was saying.

While negative body language can cancel out your verbal message, clever body language can reinforce it. Trial attorneys have long recognized that body language can be a potent weapon in the courtroom. So much so, that some lawyers hire acting coaches to teach them how to make meaningful eye contact with jurors.

Nonverbal communication is considered so effective in court cases that some judges are trying to set limits on its use.

EVERY PART OF YOU "TALKS"

Every moving part of your body "talks." Take your face, for instance: raise your eyebrows and you show surprise, or disapproval. Your eyes, the "mirror of the soul," can reveal practically anything—love, hate, horror, etc., depending on your mood. Wrinkling your forehead tells people you're confused. Scrunch up your nose and you show distaste.

The rest of your body has its own language, too. Shrugging your shoulders says "I couldn't care less"; tapping your fingers says "I'm bored, let's get this over with"; toe-tapping is a distinct signal of nervousness.

READ MY LIPS

Since *everyone* uses body language, it's important not only to control yours, but to know what others are "saying" via their bodies. It'll tell you what they're really thinking, plus help you to know how to react.

Here are some body language signals to watch out for:

Eyes averted. When someone doesn't look directly at you while you're talking, they're sending a clear message. Maybe they want to show indifference and that they don't care to listen to you. On the other hand, it may be that you're causing the problem. Perhaps you're rambling on too long and, in effect, they want to tune you out.

The far side. If you're sitting at the conference table and the person next to you shifts to the side of his or her chair that's farthest from you, slightly turning his or her back in the process, take note! That's a signal that this individual either doesn't like you or is mad at you and wants to get as far from you as possible.

Stay away. When people fold their arms in front of them, it can express anger or it may be a sign not to come too close. At any rate, it's very negative body language that demonstrates they're not open to you.

CULTURAL DIFFERENCES

Different cultures have different body language. Asians, for example, consider direct eye contact intrusive. Instead, they use a sidewards glance. In Latin America, workers keep their eyes respectfully averted when talking to the boss. Ditto for the Japanese.

Even "finger beckoning" has different meanings around the world. In America, some people curl and move the index finger to get the waiter's attention. In Australia, that's reserved for summoning "ladies of the evening." Using this gesture in

Yugoslavia and Malaysia is considered an insult. It's only used to call animals.

The A-OK sign, with the thumb and index finger joined in a circle, as well as the *V* for victory signal, have insulting and scatological connotations in many Latin American countries. Instead of signifying everything's fine, it means, "Up yours!" President Nixon learned that the hard way on his trip to Chile, when he gave his familiar victory sign.

COLOR CONSCIOUSNESS

Colors—considered an extension of body language—also give off powerful messages in the workplace. They, too, affect people's opinions of you. According to educator Ellen Olsen of the Colorado Institute of Art, "Colors . . . influence how people react to you." New employees should be particularly sensitive to the environment where they work and conscious of the colors that successful executives wear.

A lack of color consciousness can kill a career. Case in point: Charleen, a junior banking executive from the Southwest, transferred to a new job with a large Boston bank. On her first day at work she noticed a lot of the women were in somber shades of gray and blue. Thinking she would brighten up the place a bit, she decided to wear a lively purple suit and a matching blouse to an important meeting with one of the bank's biggest customers. Another time, she chose a mustard-colored suit with matching shoes to meet with the president of the bank. By then, Charleen's boss thought he had made a major mistake in hiring her. He was convinced she didn't belong. Fortunately for her, another executive took Charleen aside and explained the color facts of life—that in the conservative world of banking, neutrals are considered more appropriate. As a relative newcomer to the corporate world, Charleen had no idea she was making such a poor impression.

Nonetheless, the world would be a dreary place without color. Who wants to look like a little gray wren? Just be careful how you use your hues, especially at the office. After working for a company for a while, you can decide how much you want to stand out or blend in. The office, however, is not the place to go on a crazy color binge if you want to be taken seriously. Neutrals are usually the best choice for important business meetings. You can safely perk up a beige suit with a red blouse, for example.

The summer, however, is one season, when you can get a little looser with color. Brighter shades are much more acceptable then. According to the *New York Times*, "even men who live in gray and blue most of the time get a little adventurous with color in their summer clothes." Be aware that Easterners tend to wear darker colors year-round. The further south or west you go, the more colors lighten up, regardless of the time of year. However, if you're traveling to a meeting in the East, you'll come across as a fashion lightweight if you wear a pastel suit in the dead of winter—especially with matching shoes.

Color psychology is a science unto itself. Experts say your choice of color influences how people react to you. Here's what they say about the most common colors:

Red indicates stability and ambition. People notice you when you wear it. (When I give a speech, I always wear a red blouse with a neutral-colored suit.)

White is synonymous with innocence. Wear it when you want people to think you're trustworthy. (Go for it in the middle of summer.)

Blue indicates loyalty and honesty. The darker the shade, the more intense the emotional meaning. (Navy is the perfect color to wear when you go in for a salary review.)

Black is a power color that says you should be taken seriously. (This is my choice when I want to look in charge and won't take no for an answer.)

Green is a positive color, the shade of nature. It's comforting and healing. (In the summer, I wear it at night to business functions, never during the day.)

Yellow is often worn by upbeat, happy people. (Up to you.)

Gray is the favorite color of business. It gives the impression you're honest and serious about your job. (Listen up! This is where it's at.)

Purple is often thought of as the color of royalty. It can indicate you think you're unique and special.

Pink is a "calming" color and gives off vibes of innocence and femininity. (Experts advise wearing it if you're in a situation where you want to keep emotions under control.)

TRUE CONFESSION

After having said all of the above, I confess I love color. I like to break out in rainbow hues whenever it's appropriate, especially in the summer. One fine June morning, someone actually told me I looked like a flower (my entire outfit was pink, except for my beige shoes). Be aware, however, that I was in the kind of creative job—communications—where I was allowed some latitude. If you're in the accounting department of a large company, for example, lively colors usually won't go over too well, even in the summer. You'll have to observe others and decide for yourself what's right for your company; just be clever about your color choices.

REACHING FOR THE TOP

Your appearance can be either the bridge or the barrier to your rise to the top. It's amazing how some women will spend three hours looking for the right dress to wear to a party, and give little or no thought to dressing for the office. It's even stranger because a party lasts only one night, but the job is your *future*. Others totally ignore the effects of negative body language and wonder why their career isn't clicking quicker. Your appearance and body language are key communications channels that deserve a lot of attention and thought until you get them right. You may never be as lucky as I was to have someone whose opinion counts critique the way you look, or you may be totally oblivious to what your body language is saying. So critique yourself. Here's a quiz to help you.

QUICK QUIZ FOR GONNABE EXECUTIVES

1. Am I savvy about the way my company wants me to look?

2. Do I observe how other women at the top dress?

3. Have I pinpointed a top executive whose appearance I could imitate?

4. Have I critiqued my wardrobe lately and am I willing to chuck clothing that's too tight, too worn, or otherwise inappropriate?

5. Do people compliment my hairstyle, or do I secretly know it's wrong?

6. Are my accessories small and conservative?

7. Do I observe the basics of good grooming—daily shower or bath, deodorant, fresh breath?

8. Does my body language signal that I'm a business professional or does it say I'm not executive grade?

9. Am I alert to what other people are telling me with their body language?

10. Am I a finger-drummer, a toe-tapper, a hair-twirler, or do I control these habits?

11. Am I considerate of others' space?

12. Do I really use my eyes to convey enthusiasm, interest, concern, and comprehension?

~~~

MAX-ING YOUR MEETINGS

"For months I'd felt that the ad campaign for my company's new pet foods division was way off the mark. Although I was fairly low on the totem pole, I decided to bring it up at the weekly new products meeting. But first I had a photographer friend take some shots of my own two little puppies in heartwarming poses. I brought the photos to the meeting, explaining as I passed them around that I thought they were more in keeping with the message the company wanted to send about its product. After everyone finished ooh-ing and aah-ing, the senior account executive not only announced that he got my point, he promoted me not long after. Plus, he hired the photographer! The puppy photos are framed and displayed in my office to remind everyone of my idea. Confucius wasn't kidding when he said, 'A picture is worth a thousand words.'"

*T*his is Paula's story and a good example of how to max your meetings—how to make the most of a forum that's available in virtually every company. After all, how many times have you called a co-worker or client only to find that she or he was in a meeting? It's been estimated that the average executive spends the equivalent of one day a week in meetings of some kind, whether one-on-one with a colleague or a full-fledged conference with many people involved.

Although some executives complain that meetings are a big waste of time, these sessions are crucial to the many decisions that affect an organization. Meetings not only help managers get to know one another, they're also a great opportunity for junior team members, like Paula, to strut their stuff. Beyond that, *meetings have the power to make or break your career.*

FAIR WARNING

How you act in meetings—whether you contribute ideas or solutions for the problems at hand, or you hold back and act as if you're a nonparticipant—can be a big factor in determining if you'll move up, stay in place, or even be given your walking papers.

In my twenty-plus years working at the top for some of America's most powerful CEOs, I've been asked (*told* is more like it) to attend more meetings than I care to remember. Some were time-killers, but most unfailingly revealed who the potential winners or losers were. Somehow the people who had what it takes to succeed always emerged. They were usually a step ahead of their co-workers. Sometimes what set them apart was indefinable; maybe it was just the way they spoke and looked. Other times it was clear they were marching to the tune of a different drummer—one who obviously played better than the rest.

It always amazes me that people don't realize all meetings have a hidden agenda—and that's really to decide who's got "it" and who doesn't. Luckily, I was judged as fitting the former category. I'm convinced that my performance in some of these sessions was partially responsible for my success in business.

Meetings are one of the most meaningful venues in which you can communicate your executive abilities and leadership skills. If you take these sessions lightly, don't blame anyone else if a dark cloud settles on your career path. You've been given fair warning by the Meeting Maximizer!

PRIME PARTICIPATION

In a meeting, you can fill one of several roles—chairperson, participant, or presenter. Each role demands different skills and is equally important. Just because you're not at center stage, leading the meeting, doesn't mean that you can sit back and twiddle your thumbs.

Some women participate so poorly in meetings that they might as well not even bother to attend. They sidle in, take a faraway seat, and rarely open their mouths unless asked a direct question. If this describes your behavior, wake up! You're missing a golden opportunity to shine. Here's how to polish your performance:

1. Okay, this sounds obvious, but if you know there's an important meeting coming up, give some thought to what you're going to wear. Make sure you look bright-eyed and bushy-tailed. Instead of winging it, wardrobe-wise, maybe this is the time to pull out that snappy navy blue suit that's great for your executive image. Get up early enough to do a special job on your hair and makeup, too. Since a lot of meetings are held first thing in the morning, don't burn the midnight oil the night before. If you're still half asleep, you won't be able to give much of a performance.

2. Be there on time, if not a couple of minutes early. Arriving late sends a self-defeating signal that you think whatever you're doing is more important than the business at hand. Plus, those few minutes before the meeting starts are the prime time to do a little casual politicking. If you have to leave before the meeting ends, be sure to tell the chair that you have to exit early and when. Choose a seat near the door so you can leave unobtrusively. Catch the chairperson's eye when you go so that everyone realizes your early departure was expected. Except for that small signal to the chair, don't interrupt the meeting by saying good-bye to others; just leave quietly.

3. Before a meeting, rev up your mind by carefully reviewing your notes from the previous session as well as any material disseminated on the subject matter. Maybe it will stimulate some fresh new thinking on your part. Plus, it's very impressive to be able to say, "When we last met on April thirteenth" (it's important to give a *specific* date) "we discussed

ways to make the annual report more appealing to share-holders. Here are a few ideas that I think might work. . . ." This shows you're not only tracking the previous discussions, but you're trying to move the peanut one step further. You'd be surprised at how few people remember exactly what was discussed in prior sessions. When others realize *you* do, you give the instant impression of being on top of things.

One senior executive I worked with kept a special note-book for this purpose, jotting down significant facts from every meeting he attended. He never failed to impress people with his instant recall of who said what, and when, and, par-ticularly, which projects had been assigned to whom, and their respective due dates. Incidentally, Reuben Mark, the note-taker just described, is now the CEO of one of the largest corporations in America—Colgate-Palmolive. Take a tip from Reuben and keep a meeting notebook. It'll be one of the smartest moves you ever make.

4. Pick a seat near the action. That's usually close to the person who's heading the meeting. Try not to sit in some obscure corner where people can barely see or hear you.

5. Take the meeting as seriously as you take your pay-check. Don't joke around or waste time with frivolous dis-cussions. It's not a cocktail party!

6. Try to speak out at the beginning of the meeting, so you'll be noticed. Whatever you say doesn't have to be earth-shaking, just as long as it's pertinent.

7. Use unexpected props to make a point. Flip out a stock photo or a magazine picture, anything that illustrates your idea. It doesn't matter if the visual isn't 100 percent perfect. What you want is to have everyone associate the idea with *you*. A visual drives the point home better than anything. Save that prop and display it in a prominent place in your office. If anyone forgets who thought of the idea in the first place, just smile and point. That's what Paula's ploy was all about.

8. Always bring a pad and pen to a meeting. You'll look disorganized and unprepared if you have to borrow them from other attendees. And take notes! It shows interest and respect for other speakers. Date your notes, keep them in your meeting notebook, and be sure to review them before any follow-up meetings.

9. Don't be afraid to offer a comment on an issue that may not be connected to your own job. Let's say you're in accounting, and have been asked to attend a general meeting on the company's fourth-quarter earnings results. Mention is made of a product that's bombing, and you have some suggestions that have nothing to do with your particular area of responsibility. Don't hesitate to bring them up, as long as you do it diplomatically. The worst that can happen is that your idea might not be usable—but you'll still come off as a well-rounded person who's committed to the company's overall success, not just your own turf.

10. When the meeting ends, don't just tear out. Go over to the chairperson and tell her or him that you think the dis-

cussion was a good one. It only takes a few seconds, but it shows appreciation for the work that went into organizing the meeting. Plus, it's proper business etiquette.

OTHER PERTINENT POINTS

At meetings, people are automatically judged as either contributors or bystanders. You never want to be thought of as belonging to the latter category. Companies want *givers*, not *takers*. If you think you have little or nothing to add to a discussion, you may be wrong. Why would you have been asked to join the group in the first place? Make a promise to yourself that you'll try to find a way to comment at least once during the course of any meeting you attend, as long as group participation is encouraged (at some meetings, you're just supposed to listen).

If you don't have any ideas to contribute, you can still make yourself heard by complimenting someone else's idea. Saying something as simple as, "I like your plan, Bruce. It's creative and I think it will appeal to our customers." Or you can make your presence known by asking a question, such as, "Bruce, I like what you said. Do you think our West Coast consumers will find it too conservative?" Asking a pertinent question shows you're really into the subject that's being discussed.

When you decide to speak up, however, it's important that you do it right. Never preface your remarks with apologies like, "This may not work, but . . ." or, "You probably have thought of this already, but . . ." As I'll explain in a later chapter, negative statements like this set your idea up for failure. Always give as many *pertinent* details as you can to make your thoughts clear to everyone. Ideas lose their punch if you only drop a phrase or two and then phase out. When you're too brief, other people can glom on to *your* idea, embellish it, and try to make it *theirs*.

Another way to communicate successfully at meetings is to modulate your voice. Unfortunately, women sometimes speak so softly that it's difficult to hear them. Speak out audibly and clearly so that everyone can catch what you're saying. If you're the type who talks in little-girl whispers, you're doing yourself a disservice. You'll come across as timid and unsure of what you're saying. While it may be appealing in some social circles, it's totally inappropriate in a business setting. You'd be surprised at what increasing the volume of your voice will do for your image. It lends authority to your words in a very meaningful way. I'm not telling you to shout, but just to make sure people don't have to strain to hear you.

KEY TIPS FOR CHAIRING MEETINGS

If you're the one designated to run the meeting, you've got a great opportunity to communicate your managerial know-how regardless of the people attending. Don't blow it by giving a lackluster performance. It's flawed thinking to tell yourself, "This is only a meeting with a few co-workers, so what's the big deal?" It's important to take charge and to give any meeting you chair sufficient thought so that you will come across as organized and effective.

Here are the basics for leading a meeting:

1. If you're convening within the company, naturally you will use whatever meeting space is available. Be sure to reserve the conference room early, if there is one. If, on the other hand, you're holding the session at a hotel or other commercial venue, make sure you find a comfortable meeting room that's well lit, well ventilated, and has enough chairs.

This may sound awfully basic but you'd be surprised at how poor lighting can defeat your purpose. Information is perceived through both the ears and eyes. Poor lighting and bad ventilation tend to make people sleepy.

2. Make sure you've invited all the appropriate people. You can cause a lot of resentment by omitting someone who should have been included by virtue of her or his job status.

3. Decide well beforehand what your objectives are and what you want the meeting to accomplish. Then prepare an agenda to reflect that. Distribute it to all the attendees in advance. Agendas keep people focused. At the actual meeting, you should repeat the goals you want to achieve so everyone will understand why they are there.

4. Whenever possible, tell participants how long the meeting will last, and make sure you stick to it. Most meetings shouldn't last more than an hour. Unless there's an emergency, allowing it to run on and on is not only inconsiderate, it's usually counterproductive. People get antsy about their disrupted schedules and tend to turn off mentally. Besides,

you'll seem disorganized and incapable of running a meeting properly.

5. You can get things off to a pleasant start, particularly at a morning meeting, if you can arrange for coffee and some sort of nibbles. The simplest way to handle this is to have a set-up in a corner where everyone can help themselves. Quickly.

6. If you're going to tape-record the meeting, be sure to announce it right off the bat. Don't surprise anyone by recording their pearls of wisdom for posterity without warning them first.

7. When you use a mike, for heaven's sake test it *before* everyone arrives. A squealing mike—or one that isn't working at all—sets the tone for a bad meeting. Ditto for visuals. If you're showing slides, learn beforehand how to work the equipment. You'll look foolish if you don't. Make sure visuals are right-side up, and in the proper sequence. Uncoordinated audiovisuals can play havoc with a meeting's overall success—and make you seem ill-equipped in the leadership department.

8. Even though people presumably will be taking their own notes, give them as much prepared material as possible, particularly when statistics are involved. It's not always easy to jot down a bunch of figures accurately, and if money is involved, mistakes could be costly.

9. If the attendees are not all known to each other, it's helpful to have cards with each person's name, title, and af-

filiation, propped up on the table, facing *out*. (It doesn't do much good to have them facing each person, who certainly knows her or his own name!)

10. Unless they're comprised of heart surgeons, obstetricians, or the like, ask all participants to turn off their beeping pagers and cell phones.

11. Use your executive skills to the hilt. This begins with introducing all participants who aren't known to the rest of the group. It's also important to take charge of the meeting by not allowing others to interrupt when someone is making a point. You also should control anyone who tries to dominate the proceedings. Just say something like, "Jim, why don't we let Tish finish and then we'd like to hear from you."

As chairperson, a big part of your job is to manage the agenda. For example, if you've got five items to cover in thirty minutes, watch the clock. Allow enough time for every agenda item to be discussed. If you find any single subject is taking too long, wrap it up as best you can and move on.

12. At the end of the meeting, give a brief overall summary of what was discussed and remind participants what they're expected to do and in what time frame. It's always gracious to thank everyone for coming and to acknowledge anyone who handled any special details for the meeting. Something like, "Thanks Artie, for arranging for coffee and Deborah for preparing the slides." Again, showing good manners never hurts anyone's reputation. In fact, it helps.

The Big Tip

The previous twelve tips are just the bare bones requirements for leading a meeting. This last tip, which is the most
important thing you should do when you're chairing a meeting, I'm treating separately to make sure you don't overlook
it: Always, but *always*, distribute the minutes of a meeting as
a follow-up. Appoint a reliable person to take notes. Instruct
this individual that it's critical to list in the meeting notes the
names of everyone who has been given an assignment, and
the assignment due dates. Sometimes I print out the info in
boldfaced type so no one can claim to have missed it. In addition, I usually jot down the most important items in my
own meeting notebook in case the notetaker missed them.
Then carefully prepare these meeting notes as if your job de-
pended on it. Once you're satisfied that they accurately reflect
what was said, circulate them to all attendees.

If you fail to take minutes and are unable to recall what
actually went on, you can rightfully be accused of wasting
everyone's time. Distributing meeting notes makes all attendees accountable and reminds them of their responsibilities.
Without this written follow-up, some people might fail to follow through on their commitments and/or meet their dead-
lines. ("Gosh, I didn't understand I was supposed to do that
right away.") Their goof-off will be at your expense. After
all, *you* were chairing the meeting, so you'll have to take the
blame for any alleged miscommunication.

Chairing a meeting properly is a miniature management
exercise. Your boss, who'll probably sit in on some of the

meetings you chair, will notice how well you handle them. She or he will be making mental notes about your leadership ability. Be sure the impression you give is a positive one.

WHEN YOU'RE THE PRESENTER

If you're lucky enough to be asked to present at a meeting, be grateful. You've just been given a "leading lady" role where you can raise your visibility, display your leadership qualities, and put yourself on the fast track in one fell swoop. Here's how it might work. Let's say your company is wooing an important client. She's coming to a full-scale meeting where she'll be told of the many advantages of signing on with you, rather than with all the other firms fighting to get her business. There's a lot of money involved, plus the prestige of landing this big fish.

The entire company is in high gear, with virtually everything else put on hold to prepare for the big day—the Presentation. And you've been picked to be a presenter. You'll have fifteen minutes to fill. A quarter of an hour to pitch, persuade, push your product or service, and, hopefully, convince Ms. Important that she can't live without what you're selling.

You first need to decide on two items:

What you'll say

How you'll say it

When I was VP of Communications for Colgate-Palmolive, I presided at many such sessions, where outside agencies presented their ideas for promoting a new product or television show. The majority of these presentations were well done—crisp, to the point, and presented by people who knew how to speak, dress, and act. But some of the presentations were just plain awful. They were too long, filled with endless, boring charts, and run by people who seemed to suffer from rambling mouth disease.

One marketing firm made the fatal mistake of ignoring most of the women who were present and directing all their comments to the men on my staff. A few presenters dressed so casually they looked as if they were going to a basketball game instead of attending a serious meeting that involved hundreds of thousands of dollars. At another meeting, one of the presenters had had so much to drink before lunch that not only did he make little sense, but his boozy breath nearly blew us over. Needless to say, these firms didn't inspire a lot of confidence. They didn't get our business, either, and were never invited back.

MAKING YOUR MEETINGS MATTER

The ultimate Meeting Maximizer is my friend John Rosenwald, vice-chairman of Bear Stearns, the large and very successful investment banking company. John is a stickler for detail and for not wasting a client's time. His foresight and follow-up are famous. John can tell you not only which Yellow Brick Road to take, but how many bricks you'll be walking on. That's why the CEOs of America trust him implicitly.

When John began his career, he wasn't part of the Old Boy network and had to start at ground zero. One of the reasons for his meteoric rise to the top was that he always does his homework and insists that his staff do the same. John advises, "If a client gives me one of his most valuable commodities—his time—it's my responsibility to make the most of it. He or she doesn't need me to tell them what they already know. It's my job to come up with fresh, informative ideas and new ways of approaching a problem." Way to go, John! Anyone, at any level, female or male, can profit from your wise words.

What to Say

Unless you're the head of a huge department with several writers at your command, chances are you'll be the one responsible for putting together your presentation from start to finish. That means researching and writing it; picking out the visuals, if any; and deciding on whether to wing it, memorize it, use cards, or read a script.

When it comes to writing your presentation, follow John Rosenwald's advice: tell them what they don't already know. Also try to find a way not to bore your audience. I once sat through a morning meeting at Colgate-Palmolive in which each division head had to give a mini-briefing on the current status of his group's activities. Now these guys (yes, they *were* all guys) were fairly adept at making presentations, but some were clearly better than others. The men who really made an impression were clear, upbeat, to the point, and brief. Others who didn't fare so well either had no energy in their voices, used dull graphics, or were about as exciting as watching paint dry.

I remember this particular presentation because one sad soul made a poor impression before he even opened his mouth. Somehow Paul, from one of the company's subsidiaries, didn't sufficiently pick up on the executive dress code and showed up in a loud-checked jacket, a flashy multi-print tie and khaki pants. He stood out like a sore thumb among the other nineteen vice-presidents, all of whom were in well-tailored navy or gray suits, with conservative ties, shirts, and shoes. As we all listened to Paul's presentation we found it hard to take him seriously because he looked so out of place.

The standout presenter at the meeting was my pal David Seiniger, who ran the Marisa Christina fashion division for us. David, who had a wicked sense of humor, was not about to stand up and bore his audience. He knew that showing some statistics was mandatory, but to grab his audience's attention right off the bat, he opted not to show the typical slides of the manufacturing plant and the production line. Instead, he ran photos of beautiful Eurasian models (the plant was located in Hong Kong) wearing the new line, each holding flash cards depicting the sales orders that had come in from Saks, Neiman Marcus, Bloomingdale's, etc. He didn't have to say a word about his division's bottom line; his photos told the story. Every guy there certainly thought so, too!

REHEARSAL

Treating your presentation as if it's just another day at the office is a sure way to invite disaster. Even if you're speaking for just a few minutes, make them golden, by the simple device of rehearsing.

One of the oldest jokes in the Western world concerns a tourist in New York who has lost his way. He approaches a passerby and asks, "Excuse me, how do I get to Carnegie Hall?" To his surprise, the response he gets is: "Practice, practice, practice!"

Even if you're not a violin virtuoso, those are still words of wisdom. The ideal way to rehearse, of course, is to put it on tape. If you have a camcorder (or can rent one), this is the perfect way to—as the poet Robert Burns put it—"see ourselves as others see us." If for some reason this isn't a possibility, the next best thing, of course, is to rehearse in front of a mirror. Just make sure it's full-length; your audience will be seeing more of you than just your head.

Force yourself to include *all* the body movements you plan to make—hand gestures, nods, eye contact, etc. This kind of verbal and visual rehearsal will help you see how you'll appear to your audience.

PRESENTATION POINTERS

When you're going to pitch to a group, whether it's your own management, a client, or whomever, be sure to keep in mind the following few basics:

1. Prepare your visual and verbal strategies *very* carefully. This is definitely not the time to "wing it."

2. Ask yourself, "What's in this for the person I'm pitching to?" and then make sure you deliver it.

3. If you had to distill your message into a single sentence, what would it be? Always make sure you don't stray too far from this central theme.

4. Once you decide on your key message, get to it as quickly as you can.

5. Choose the simplest way you can to state your goals. Don't confuse people with fancy words and convoluted sentences, thinking you'll sound smarter. You won't fool anyone. Listen to how it sounds if you say, "We made a corporate decision to interpose in all advertising the new, improved mechanisms in William's Widgets and their lack of interstitial imperfections, as well as the basic elements of installation and long-term usage," versus "We plan to have our advertising focus on the ease of using the new, improved William's Widgets."

6. Before you get up and present, give yourself a pep talk. Say to yourself: "I am intelligent, I know what I'm talking about, and these people are not my enemies waiting for me to fall on my face."

7. Always be prepared for Q&A. If you're not sure of the answer, say so. No one is required to know everything; there's nothing wrong with replying: "Sorry, I don't have the answer

right now, but I'll find out and get back to you." (And then make sure you do.)

8. At the end of the meeting, briefly sum up the important points and decisions that have been made and any follow-up action required by specific individuals.

9. Use your executive manners: thank people for coming and listening, compliment anyone who assisted you, and so on.

10. Lastly, always remember you probably won't die if your pitch fails. Everyone strikes out on occasion.

Wrap Up

Unfortunately, not everyone takes meetings as seriously as they should. At one meeting I attended, "Sherry" unthinkingly pulled out her blush and lipstick and did a quick touch-up (too girly!). At another, "Barry" obviously had spent too much time partying the night before and could barely keep his eyes open. At a very important sales meeting, "Carla," in her efforts to impress everyone, interrupted the speakers so frequently that she made a real pest of herself. These three individual's goofs may have been minor, but they show that all of them lost sight of the important fact that they were on view and that their performance was being judged.

The best advice I can give you if you want to score meeting points is to pretend that a meeting is like a job interview, where you know you must be on your best behavior. Would you put on lipstick there, or close your eyes for a few seconds and rest? Hardly! Everything you do and say in a meeting is subject to scrutiny. Never take them casually. Your participation, whether you're chairing, presenting, or just listening, is always being judged. Always remember you're like a bug under a microscope where higher-ups are scoping out your management potential. Meetings can be a showcase for success or a platform for failure.

three

WORKING A ROOM

HAPPY HOLIDAYS!

"The annual Christmas party fell on a night when I had been with the company only two weeks, as an entry-level junior accountant. Although I hardly knew anyone, I had been taught in college to always 'work the room,' so I dashed around and chatted with anyone who would talk to me. I received a warm reception, thanks in part to my new red suit, which I thought I looked terrific in, although it cost me an arm and a leg.

"I accidentally knocked the arm of a well-dressed, self-assured man at the buffet table, so I apologized and began talking to him. I told him I had just taken a job as a junior accountant with the company. He said that he, too, had begun his career in accounting.

" 'Then you might be interested in a funny thing that happened today,' I said. 'I was looking at the first-quarter projection figures, and they seemed out of whack. Much too high. I thought maybe an extra zero had been entered. I tried to tell my boss, but she wouldn't even look at them. She said projection figures came down from the president's office, and were sacrosanct.'

" 'What was the figure?' he asked. I told him. 'You made a good catch, young woman,' he replied. 'Someone indeed held his finger on the zero key an instant too long, and it struck twice.'

"He gave me a big smile, asked my name, and said, 'You'll go far in this company.' Then he winked and added, 'Don't worry, I won't tell your boss you went over her head.'

"A moment later, after the man had left, a woman from my department ran up to me and said, 'You must really have hit it off with the CEO for him to spend so much time talking to you. He's usually very reserved.' I was flabbergasted and felt like a dummy for not recognizing him, and I was sure I was going to get in trouble with my boss.

"Just the opposite happened! Believe it or not, four months later I was given a big promotion and a fat raise. I never told anyone about my 'accidental' conversation with the CEO. I stayed with the company for the next ten years, eventually becoming financial vice president of my division."

Yes, Virginia, there is a Santa Claus! This merry tale was told to my friend, Don Softness, one of the country's leading communications practitioners who repeated it to me. As incredible as it sounds, Don swears it actually happened to a colleague of his. It's such a great anecdote I had to share it with you because it illustrates the very best of what could happen when you're "working the room." It doesn't always turn out this well, but, hey, you never know!

Not everyone is as fearless as Don's friend. Walking into a room alone, particularly when it's full of strangers who can influence your career or boost your social life, is very intimidating to most people. If just thinking about it makes your heart thump and your palms sweat, you're not alone. This kind of social anxiety is very real—and perfectly normal. Knowing that may give you comfort, but it doesn't make it any easier. What woman doesn't wish she could do it better? Why can't you be the one who glides into the XYZ sales conference and is adored, admired, and praised by all? Wouldn't it be nice if every time you "worked" a room you made a new business contact or met someone who could put your social life in high gear? Wish no more! This chapter is going to give you the secrets of savvy socializing so that you can jump-start your career and life.

WHAT TO DO?

Imagine this scenario: Your boss tells you that you've been selected to go to the company's annual sales conference. Besides all the business sessions you're supposed to attend, you're required to be at the cocktail party that kicks off the meetings. Of course you're complimented by the invitation. Then you start thinking about how important it is that you make a good impression, particularly on the business bigwigs who'll be at the party. What do you say to them that not only is halfway intelligent, but makes you stand out in their minds?

The very first thing you should do is psyche yourself up. Tell yourself you're going to have a good time and that you'll make the most of the occasion. Just saying these things to yourself can help change your attitude. Walking into a room when you're full of energy and self-confidence will get you a lot further than inching in with fear frozen on your face.

The next thing to do is to sit back and ask yourself what you'd like to accomplish. What's your goal? When you leave the event, what would you like to see happen? Whatever your answer is, that's your *E.O. (event objective)*. Be very deliberate in asking and answering these questions. It's important that you go through this mental exercise *beforehand* so you'll have a clear vision of what your event objective is. Without it, you won't get much out of any occasion.

FUN, FUN, FUN!

It's perfectly okay if your purpose isn't noble. Maybe you just want to have fun. After all, who wants to have a lousy time? But along with enjoying yourself, you could just as easily accomplish other things. For example, maybe you've made a New Year's resolution to find another job. Then that's your E.O. Try to meet and chat up people who might be in a position to help you. Or maybe your goal is to introduce yourself to your company's regional VP and have him think you're the best thing since America went on-line. Having an event objective keeps you on track and helps you work a room to maximum effectiveness.

YOUR NAME ISN'T OPRAH

Your next challenge is to find a way to meet people, especially those you want to get to know better. Unless you're

Oprah, or you've just won the lottery, you can't just sit back and wait for people to come over and introduce themselves to you. Get with it and introduce yourself. The best introductions take no more than ten seconds, and include your name, what you do, plus a few more facts that will help people remember you. If you're at a business function, it could go something like this: "Hi, I'm Jennifer Connors, and I work in accounting. I hear you're a Steelers fan [or whatever else you've heard, as long as it's positive], I am too!" If nothing else, you can always mention the weather: "Isn't this sunshine fabulous?" Anything to get the conversation going. Don't feel you just have to talk about business. Everybody enjoys a break from the daily grind.

Don't hesitate to be the first to say hello. When my friend Dale meets anyone new she always gives them a big smile and a firm handshake—whether the person's male or female. She says the firm part is critical; it shows self-confidence. I think Dale's got something going here; people naturally remember you better if you greet them in a friendly way.

OPENING LINES

Lots of gals get hung up trying to think of a great opening line. When they can't dredge one up, they don't bother saying anything. There's no such thing as the perfect opener. Even if you say something that you think sounds sort of silly, it's better than nothing at all. Believe me—it doesn't take all that much to get a conversation going. Deals have been made, jobs have been offered, and social relationships launched by relatively simple, everyday remarks. Even asking someone what time it is has been known to get things moving.

Never hesitate to start with your name, even if you think the other person probably recognizes you. Lew Rudin, a real estate mogul, long acknowledged as one of New York's most popular power brokers and effective "room-workers," always makes a point of giving his name when he says hello. Unless he knows the other person extremely well, he invariably mentions his name in the same breath that he greets her or him. He advises, "Why make it hard for someone to recognize you? No one is so important that they can't give their name when saying hello."

When you meet someone new, force yourself to smile (this is obviously *far* better than a blank face or a nervous frown), make eye contact, and say your name clearly. At this point, most people will give you theirs in return, and then a conversation can begin. If someone is rude enough not to offer their name, just ask. Better to do that than let them get away with it. Besides, you need the information. Use some small talk to warm up the dialogue. Ask about their golf or tennis game, their job, talk about the next day's session, etc. Don't pooh-pooh small talk just because it's superficial. It serves a purpose. It paves the way for big talk, and it breaks the ice. Once you've cracked through, you can talk about whatever it is you really want to discuss.

My friend Pat Nation, a well-respected newspaper journalist, is known for her uncanny ability to waltz around a room and somehow always meet the movers and shakers who are there. The way she does it is by using what she calls the "candy box" technique. "If someone gives you a box of candy, most people pick and choose their favorites before they gobble them down," she says. "It's the same with meeting people. I know I don't have all night, so I carefully select the ones I want to spend time talking with. I deliberately don't chat with people I know well, unless I haven't seen them in a long time. Instead, I just wave hello and then make a beeline for anyone in the room whom I don't know or who looks shy or adrift. I've met fabulous people this way and had terrific conversations.

"Most people think they have to wait to be introduced to bigwigs. I don't think this is always true. If you're there and they're there, why chance not meeting someone just because you've never formally met? For example, I once walked up to Prince Philip, no less, at a party and had a great chat with him about horse racing. I think my genuine interest in meeting new people eliminates the necessity of waiting for a 'proper introduction'—which may never happen," Pat concludes.

BREAKING AWAY

You must also know how to break away from someone whose company doesn't interest you. No one ever said you have to be a martyr and remain stuck to the floor just to be nice. You don't need elaborate excuses to end a conversation. Just a simple "Excuse me, it's been great talking to you, but I need to speak to someone else" or "I see my husband [colleague, boss, etc.] and I want to say hello." Then make sure when you walk away that you *do* say hello to someone so your excuse makes sense. Be careful with the old line about getting yourself another drink. The person you're trying to dump (especially if it's a male) may just say, "Oh, I'll be happy to get you one. What would you like?" Then you're stuck for another twenty minutes.

If it's a business occasion, especially if the person is obviously senior to you, be sure the words you use to exit are deferential to her or his stature. You can always say, "I don't want to monopolize your time. I just wanted to say hello."

LISTEN UP

While you're doing all this mixing and mingling, make sure you've developed the art of being a dedicated listener. Listening well is not so simple. It's one of the most difficult interpersonal tasks to master. Think about some of your recent conversations. How often did you interrupt while the other person was in the middle of a point? Did you pay attention to what was being said, or were you too busy planning your next comment—or letting your mind wander? Listening well and staying on track isn't easy.

If you want to make a really good impression, just remember a good rule of thumb is to listen 80 percent of the time and talk 20 percent. People can't help but be flattered when you're all ears and giving them your full, rapt attention. One way to show you're listening up is to use your face to acknowledge that you're tracking the conversation. Nodding, smiling, and maintaining eye contact all demonstrate that you're following what's being said.

If your mind starts wandering and you're really not listening, here's a little trick the pros use: Start repeating silently to yourself whatever the other person is saying. This helps bring your attention back to the speaker.

Make it your business to be an active, not a passive, listener. Just staring dreamily into someone's eyes while you're really thinking about something else isn't enough. Active listening means *hearing* what the other person is saying—taking in their words and then giving feedback. Your response needn't be mind-boggling, just something that shows you're paying attention. It could be as simple as, "Yes, I agree. Do you think everyone feels the same?" There's a payoff to all this. When you really concentrate on what the other person is saying and react with interest, your chances of making a positive impression are a zillion times better.

If you want to be a better listener, here are other ways to do it:

1. *Understand that good listening skills are key to survival in business.* Information is power; you'll need plenty of it in order to succeed in business. One of the best (and easiest) ways to get information is by paying close attention to what is being said. Picking up vital information can really be as simple as that.

2. *Stop talking!* If you overspeak and constantly interrupt, you'll be sending a clear signal that you're not listening to what the other person is saying. Talker beware!

3. *Refocus your attention*. Everyone wants to appear bright-eyed, bushy-tailed, and full of fascinating facts to convey. However, if you want to really improve communications with others, make them the full focus of your attention. Concentrate more on listening to what *they* have to say rather than on just giving *your* opinion or trying to drop pearls of wisdom. Deliberately ask questions to keep the other person talking. Most will be flattered by your interest. (I know I would.)

4. *Realize that good listening skills require hard work*. Experts say that we listen at a rate of 480 words per minute, but that the average person only talks at a rate of 120 words per minute. Be careful, because this discrepancy gives your mind plenty of time to wander. Curb this tendency by deliberately concentrating and expanding in your mind the points the other person is trying to make. Otherwise, you'll be a victim of mental wanderlust, and you might just miss out on something important.

5. *Learn to listen with your eyes*. One of the most negative things you can do when you're in the listener mode is to break eye contact. If you look away or around the room, it tells the other person you're obviously not paying attention and what they have to say is not that important to you.

6. *Watch your other nonverbal messages*. If you're not careful, your silent messages may inadvertently make people think you're not interested in what they're saying. Gestures like frowning, tapping your fingers, glancing at your wrist-

watch, or not leaning forward all communicate that you don't care to listen. You express far more interest in the other person when you pull toward the conversation. Sitting or standing like a statue sends a totally negative message. Behavior like this will make the speaker feel not only put down, but ripe for retaliation.

7. *Suspend judgment.* Even if you think what the other person is saying is a bunch of hooey, keep on listening. Being a good listener means remembering that we all have different realities, and that the other person's message is *his* truth and has value to *him.* So listen up, you might learn something.

8. *Remember that good conversation is a two-way street.* Someone who *just* listens and never opens her mouth is as big a bore as the overtalker. While it's very important to listen well, it's equally important to respond to the person who's talking.

9. *Listening by itself is not enough.* Listening is only half the battle. You must also remember what's being said. However, that requires selectivity; otherwise you'll be in verbal overload. Some people retain information easier than others. If you're not one of those fortunate few, key into the important points you've just heard and write them down as soon as possible. My friend Patricia Francy, treasurer of New York's Columbia University, told me that if she's not going back to the office after attending a business function, she immediately calls her answering machine to leave a message for herself about any salient facts that might have been men-

tioned. That way she knows for sure she won't forget any important matters that were discussed, as well as any follow-up expected of her.

10. *Concentrate more on listening than on preparing an instant response.* Too many of us are so busy worrying about what we're going to say next that we often miss much of what the other person is telling us. Instead of feeling you have to come up with an immediate response that equals theirs, you can communicate far more effectively if you hear the other person out first, ask more questions, and then respond.

SAILING SOLO

The best way to mix and mingle at cocktail parties is to move around solo. Even if you come to the party with some-one, make the rounds by yourself. Having a friend in tow dilutes the impression you might make. Just say to whomever you came with, "Let's split up so we can network." If you're part of a twosome, people don't get as good a chance to know you personally. Plus, people are usually hesitant to offer ad-vice, help with your career, or give a compliment in front of a third person. Besides, if you're batting a thousand, and someone gives you a few nifty job ideas, why share them with anyone else?

BUSINESS CARDS READY-TO-GO

Let's say you've just had a successful conversation and you want to cement the relationship. What to do? The best ammunition is your business card. Don't ever leave home without them! Have them handy so you can zip one out. There's nothing worse than digging around in your purse to find your card. If you take too long, the other person is likely to say, "Don't bother, Bettina! Just mail it to me." Bad mistake! You've just lost the energy of communication.

Writing your name and number on a wet cocktail napkin is no substitute, either. It makes you seem disorganized. When you get home, jot notes on the backs of any business cards you've just collected while specifics are still fresh in your mind. Because it's easy to lose a business card, it's better to enter the names and phone numbers of any people you want to follow up with in your address book.

If you don't have business cards, either because you haven't yet reached that level or you are between jobs, get some! You can have them printed inexpensively at a photocopy store or buy software and make them on your computer. The cards should include your name, company, title (if any), and phone and fax numbers. If you're between jobs, print up cards with your home information.

"Working a room" is all about networking. In the competitive '90s and beyond, you need to be able to communicate *personally* who you are and what you do. "Working a room" effectively is like taking out a personal ad and not having to pay for it. It can be one of the cheapest and easiest ways to sell yourself. If you follow the strategies in this chapter, you should be able to create a little moonglow wherever you go. Make the most of it!

WRAP UP

When preparing to go to your next business function, resolve that you will use these winning strategies:

- Stop the queasies by psyching yourself up.

- Fasten onto a goal—your event objective.

- Walk up to people and introduce yourself.

- Start a conversation about anything, the weather, the decor, or even the food.

- Brush off losers with a little white lie.

- Be an active listener.

- Make the rounds by yourself.

- Have your business cards at your fingertips.

TALK LIKE A MAN, THINK LIKE A WOMAN

"A business colleague and I were driving to a meeting. As we approached a deli, I asked him if he was hungry. He said no, and kept on driving. After I expressed my annoyance, he said, 'I'm sorry. I didn't understand that you were hungry. I thought you were asking if I was.' Huh? How could he miss what I was saying? Later I figured it out. Instead of expressing my request directly (as most men would have done if they were hungry), I'd hinted at it. After all, that's what women are taught to do instead of saying what's really on their minds."

This actually happened to me years ago but I still remember it vividly. It's typical of the indirect way women sometimes speak, which carries over into major as well as minor situations. Exactly why do we women persist in talking like women in situations where our very success often depends on talking like a man? Yes, that question might sound sexist—but is it? You'd have to be living in a cave not to realize that the culture of business, for the most part, is male-oriented. A man's way of speaking and acting is the accepted norm. This is understandable when you consider that *everyone*, men and women alike, has to adapt to whatever the prevailing culture is if they want to get along. Ask any guy who's ever been in the army if he didn't have to learn real fast to "talk the talk and walk the walk" in order to survive. Why should it be any different for women when they enter the workforce?

THINKING LIKE A WOMAN

For one thing, most women are conditioned from childhood to speak in a decidedly different style than men. Bragging about ourselves is a real no-no, for instance. Consequently, it's more comfortable for us to put ourselves down than to sing our own praises. Most businessmen, on the other hand, haven't the slightest problem telling you how well they handled a project, how effective their ideas were, and so on.

Females are also brought up to seek approval, closeness, and friendship. Bossiness and aggressiveness are not traits most little girls are taught to cultivate in themselves. Consequently, we learn early on to speak indirectly, be modest, ask rather than order, and never say exactly what we're thinking. Inevitably, these ingrained habits affect both our business behavior and our personal lives.

This has its advantages and disadvantages. In childhood, women are taught to be considerate of other people's feelings. This serves them well in the business world, as women are frequently acknowledged to have better interpersonal skills than their male counterparts. This is all part and parcel of thinking like a woman.

Men, unlike women, were not taught to focus on other people's sensitivities. Rather, they have been programmed to say it like it is, regardless of the effect it may have on others. Consequently, their speech is often more forceful and straightforward.

For example, experts say women unlike men tend to avoid direct words like "would" or "will you," and substitute "could" or "can you" instead. Listen to how different "*could* you" is from "*would* you." Using the word "could" implies the other person has a choice, that he or she can comply or not, whereas the word "would" is a directive. If you still don't get it, how about "*Would* you marry me?" versus "*Could* you marry me?"

MALESPEAK

Let's consider the business world, an environment that's dominated by male values. If you try hinting or beating around the bush to make your point there, you'll get nowhere fast. Herein lies the dilemma. Women are suddenly plunged into a world where the way they were taught to speak works against them. Given this dichotomy, how *should* we talk? Do we chuck our childhood training and adopt malespeak?

Yes and no. When we're in professional situations with male colleagues—which seems to be 99 percent of the time— it makes much more sense to speak the way men do. This doesn't mean you have to become rough and tough, and spew out four-letter words—that's not the language of business either. You also don't have to lose your femininity or individuality. It *does* mean that when you communicate you have to "follow the leader." In a male-dominated culture, deviation from the norm of acceptable communication not only doesn't cut it, it can sabotage your career.

FROM WIMP TO WINNER

In countless conversations in business, many women undermine their authority and lessen their credibility without even knowing why. For starters, some women have a habit of using wishy-washy expressions that make them sound unsure of what they're talking about. Others are guilty of "overspeak," taking forever to get to the heart of the matter and causing others to lose interest. I've known quite a few females whose flowery expressions and overdramatizations made them appear silly and unbusinesslike to their male co-workers. While none of these habits will get you fired, they won't get you promoted either.

There are many ways a woman can sabotage her career when communicating. Here are some of the most common:

• **Discounting**. Women frequently denigrate their ideas by starting off with a disclaimer: "This may sound dumb, but . . ." or "You've probably thought of this already, but . . ." or "I don't know if this makes any sense, but . . ." When you use these expressions, you water down the importance of what you're saying. Instead of coming off as modest (a trait most women were taught to value), you come across as insecure. Plus, you diminish your authority and give the listener a good excuse to discount your message. You're also indirectly encouraging your colleague to think it really may *be* a dumb idea rather than a perfectly valid one. Yes, it's confusing and contradictory to the way you may have been brought up, but that's the way it is. The "world" of business is just that—it's another country, another place, and you must adopt its communications values if you intend to succeed.

• **Apologizing**. Linguistic experts say women apologize far more than men in the workplace, causing them to appear more blameworthy and less authoritative. Because many women feel personally responsible for most of what goes wrong in life, they wind up apologizing for things they have little or absolutely no control over—like the weather. "I'm so sorry you had to visit our company on such a nasty day." There's a difference between expressing genuine concern and apologizing when there's no need to. It's not necessary to make yourself the fall guy for things that aren't your responsibility. Although you won't get boiled in oil for it, always assuming blame—even for little things—subtly diminishes your credibility. After one apology too many, people may start to think you're a "goof-up" who can't do anything right.

• **Verbal gymnastics**. Some women have a habit of "walking their voice up" at the end of a sentence. As a result, they seem to be asking a question instead of making a statement. If you're guilty of this, it makes you sound doubtful or not sure of what you're saying. To put more authority and punch into your voice, lower your pitch when you end a sentence.

• **Overspeaking.** Some women are affected by what I call "rambling mouth disease." They think they have to go into every little detail in order for their listener to understand what they're talking about. As a result, they drone on and on while the other person fidgets and wonders if they'll ever get to the point.

Whenever you're making a report, hit the heart of the matter first, then give the extraneous details. In business, it's called an "executive summary." First summarize the matter at hand and then add the frills if necessary. You want to sell the "steak," not the "sizzle." I'm reminded of the TV show *Dragnet*, in which the lead character, Sergeant Friday, had a signature phrase: "Just the facts, ma'am. Just the facts." Dear old Sergeant Friday was making a point: Some women (and men, too) go beyond the facts and add so many details that the listener loses both interest and patience. My advice to you is to look 'em straight in the eye and speak your piece. Keep your sentences short and make your point as quickly as you can.

• **Filling the silence.** When you're in a meeting, who says you have to be the one to chitter-chatter just because no one else is saying anything? You have absolutely *no* obligation to fill the silence with the sound of your voice. Seldom do men find it necessary to do so. Besides, when you speak impromptu like this, you're liable to say something that makes you sound silly. A business meeting is not a cocktail party, and it's not *your* job to keep the conversation moving. If there are quiet moments, go with the flow instead of jumping in with yakety-yak. You're a businesswoman, not a geisha. It's not your responsibility to entertain everyone.

• **Speed-talking**. The best communicators speak between 140 and 170 words per minute. Certainly, not *every* woman is guilty of talking too fast, but if you are, slow down. It's irritating to others when you talk too fast. You not only lose credibility, but eventually you'll lose whomever you're talking to because they won't be able to follow what you're saying.

• **Going overboard**. "That was a good presentation," Walter said. "It was absolutely unbelievable and so beautifully thought out," commented his colleague, Connie. Walter was talking the way he usually does, restrained and right to the point. Connie spoke as she usually does, too—effusive and gushy. Her review of the presentation sounded almost as if she were describing a work of art. There is nothing wrong with what either of them said. The only difference is that Walter used manspeak, which is generally bare bones, and Connie used womanspeak, which traditionally is lengthier and employs a fistful of adverbs and adjectives ("intensifiers") to make the same point. Experts say that these intensifiers actually weaken or diminish a statement. They're considered "too emotional" and unbusinesslike. Don't fall into this trap. Try to minimize your use of intensifiers in both your conversation and your written communiqués—memos, reports, letters, etc. If you like using such verbiage, save it for social situations.

ADAPTING YOUR WAY OF SPEAKING

Male-female communications differences such as the above are everyday occurrences. That they exist and can cause problems for women in business is obvious. However, the solution is fairly simple. All that's required of you is what psychologists call "adaptive communications." More directly put, it means speaking in the language that's appropriate to the culture you're in. For example, if you take a trip to Mars, you'll need to speak Martian if you want to get your point across clearly. It's the same for business. If you want to succeed, speak the way that's acceptable to those you want to impress—the power people. Need I say more?

PROTECTING YOUR EXECUTIVE IMAGE

All of the preceding discussion is part and parcel of projecting and protecting your executive image. Now what in blazes is *that* supposed to mean? Don't *all* savvy, college-educated career women communicate and conduct themselves like full-fledged executives? Sadly, the answer is no. Despite the tremendous gains women have made at junior and middle-level jobs, too many of us damage our cause by blithely ignoring the set-in-stone fact that male values still rule the roost. Simply put, work is organized by men based on *their* psychological view of the world and the behavior *they* think is appropriate.

It shouldn't come as a complete surprise that the very top levels of the corporate world are basically an exclusive men's club. A recent article in *Business Week* revealed these startling statistics: In the five hundred largest corporations in America, only 2.4 percent of top-tier positions are held by women! And even among those few females who are CEOs of major companies, three out of five lucked into their leadership spots through spousal death or parental inheritance. Although it may be a slow dance to the top for women, there are many things you can do to improve your status, whether you're a junior executive or on the verge of shattering that infamous glass ceiling.

Although conventional wisdom is that business is ruled by an exclusionary cabal of males who are inherently determined to keep women out of top jobs, there are a growing number of exceptions. While many males *are* exclusionary, preferring to pass the leadership baton to someone similar to themselves, many others are open to helping women move up the ladder. But there is an all-important caveat: those women not only have to be eminently qualified—they must exhibit executive-style behavior around the clock.

There are a hundred and one ways to act like an executive—male or female—but let's concentrate on the special challenges that women face. Many methods can help you demonstrate that you're ready to take your place in the executive suite. Here are some of the best:

• **Avoid deep victories**. In their intense desire to prove themselves, many women think their victories must be clear-cut and public. In their minds, there must be no doubt *they* were right and *someone else* was wrong. If it's a guy who's goofed, be extra careful how you convey this idea. Like it or not, you're *really* treading on dangerous ground when you criticize a man. If you're foolish enough to do it in front of others, watch out for the inevitable knife in your back. Men *hate* to lose, especially to a woman.

Avoid bloody victories in general, but particularly over your male counterparts. Learn to score with subtlety and let others off the hook gracefully, even when you know they're wrong. That's what smooth, successful male operators do.

• **Don't be territorial.** Don't defend to the death your responsibilities as outlined in your job description. Some women, afraid they'll be taken advantage of, are very resentful when they're asked to do anything that's the slightest bit beyond the parameters of their job. When you're asked to do something extra—do it! Your boss may just be testing you to see if you can handle other responsibilities. That's one of the reasons I became the first female VP in the two-hundred-year history of the multibillion-dollar Colgate-Palmolive Company.

One day the CEO, to whom I reported, gave me an almost impossible assignment: Arrange a complicated press conference in London with only a few days notice. Aside from this being a humongous assignment, it also involved several elements that had nothing to do with my job directly. I didn't mention a word about this to him. I just took it as part of what I was asked to do and did it. This involved contacting over two hundred people, persuading them to attend, and obtaining passports for more than a dozen speakers. Plus, I had to develop presentations and press materials. I managed to pull it off—with my staff's help—and it turned out to be one of the company's most successful press conferences ever.

Months later, the CEO remarked that, at the time, even *he* wasn't sure whether his request could be fulfilled successfully. He also said he was amazed at how calm I remained throughout the ordeal, especially when he knew he was asking me to do things I wasn't familiar with. When I was elected corporate vice-president, the CEO recalled that the way I tackled and ran with the London press conference had convinced him of what he already knew—that I was ready for a major promotion.

Don't worry about being taken advantage of if you're asked to handle something that's not part of your usual job. You'll be smart enough to recognize and call a halt to it if it gets out of hand. And speaking of going beyond the call of duty, always try to do favors for your co-workers. That's how you build a cadre of fellow executives who might fight for you someday— or at least refrain from knifing you in the back.

• **Learn how to be indispensable.** Some Generation Xers have an irritating sense of entitlement and don't realize they have to earn their stripes in the working world. Instead of focusing on what they should *give* to the job in order to advance, they concentrate solely on what they can *get* from it. Along the lines of what JFK said—"Ask not what your country can do for you, ask what you can do for your country"— one way to demonstrate you care about your job is to make a real effort to anticipate your boss's needs even before she or he makes the request. Find out what she *really* wants—not merely what she *says* she wants, or what the management manual says she *ought* to want—and then deliver. This isn't a phony-baloney "butter 'em up." technique. It's a a genuine desire to do your very best and pay your dues in the process.

• **Don't be afraid to be a lone wolf.** Many women feel comfortable only when working in a group—as part of a team. No successful company was ever run by committee, nor did a group ever become CEO. When the situation warrants, take the bull by the horns and go it alone. That's one way to demonstrate leadership potential. But all the while keep on networking—not just with co-workers but with higher-ups as well.

• **Ask for your rewards.** Men routinely ask for raises and other benefits—far more than women do. As I said in *The Savvy Woman's Success Bible*, women are often too willing to settle for compliments ("You're doing a great job, Jane") instead of cash. But timing is everything. Know when to ask—and that's *not* when the company or your boss is in a down cycle.

• **Give up on Prince Charming.** Society has always taught women that without a man they're like half a pair of scissors. Too many women don't feel truly successful unless their love life is equal to their job status. On the other hand, society assumes a man is successful regardless of whether he's divorced, happily married, or has a mistress. Women must learn that their success in business has nothing to do with whether they're single, divorced, or married to their prince.

• **Want it badly enough.** Companies demand a life of sacrifice from their upwardly mobile executives. Count on missed dinners, ruined weekends, canceled vacations, and continual travel. Companies want more than superior performance, they want total dedication, too.

• **Avoid misreading the company**. Too many women think a company has a soul. They'd like a corporation to psychically put its arms around them and tell them how much they care. Men, because they've been around longer, know this isn't going to happen. They understand that a company can't coddle its employees. Rarely, if ever, will anyone give you a pep talk when you're down or tell you that you have the potential to be great and then show you how to do it. After all, this isn't nursery school. While many corporations have become family-friendly in recent years (offering maternity/paternity leave, etc.), money is still the bottom line. If you're on a fast track, you'll live a life of compromises: not enough time with your family and tension with your significant other. Expect it!

If all this seems like Management 101, you're right. You'd be surprised, however, at how many capable women overlook the obvious because, unlike men, no one has ever coached them in the basics. Despite having all the right credentials—education, dedication, and excellent job skills—many women still don't make it to the top. A lot of the time it's simply because they fail to note the B.G.O. of Life—the Blinding Glimpses at the Obvious.

≈

SOCIALIZING FOR SUCCESS

"We seem to be in the middle of an outbreak of niceness. Giving money and time to charity is on the rise too. As the population ages, we're in for more niceness."

That's what Forbes magazine has to say about the revival of good behavior. And *Variety*, the show business Bible, also acknowledges the return of good manners, even in macho Hollywood: "Rudeness is no longer a way of life in Hollywood as it was in the '80s. Civility is in."

Remember those fuddy-duddy words, "please" and "thank you"? Well, they're back! After decades of turning a blind eye to rudeness and social gaffes, it's as if our universe came to a screeching halt and said, "Enough already!"

In the dog-eat-dog '80s, manners fell by the wayside. Now, in the nicer '90s, businesspeople are clamoring for clues about executive etiquette. They're devouring books, newspapers, and magazine columns that tell you what's proper and what's not. Business executives are even attending etiquette seminars and buying instructional videos like never before. There seems to be an aggressive commitment to being nice, especially in the workplace, where *nice* used to be a dirty word. Cutthroat Island has given way to Polite Peninsula!

All of this makes perfect sense. For any businessperson to be successful, one needs all the people skills one can muster. That, in essence, is what manners are: treating others with respect and consideration. It's no wonder the manners movement seems to be multiplying faster than fat-free foods on the supermarket shelves.

ARE YOU A CLUELESS KLUTZ?

So what's all this got to do with you? Plenty! Your manners—or the lack of same—telegraph a very clear message about who and what you are. They quickly label you as either a savvy socializer or a clueless klutz. Many a wannabe executive can't make the cut because she lacks the social polish to take her to the top. Sister Friend, rest assured—etiquette goes far beyond taking a quick course in charm school. Manners are a set of golden guidelines for everyday living. Politeness not only makes the world a kinder, gentler place, but showing it helps you project the polished image of a *gonnabe* executive.

SOCIAL KNOW-HOW

None of this is surprising, considering the fact that executives have always been judged, at least in part, by their social skills. These days, however, business etiquette carries even more weight, with the ever-increasing tendency to mix social and business activities. Nowadays, success in business depends almost as much on social skills as technical know-how. This chapter is meant to give you a bird's-eye view of etiquette, with emphasis on the necessary niceties for the workplace. You can bone up on all the other social extras by reading a book like *New Manners for the '90s*, by my extraordinarily talented friend, Letitia Baldrige.

DINING OUT

Not so long ago, most children learned table manners at their mother's knee. Now, with the proliferation of working women, and the subsequent disappearance of the daily family meal, table manners have literally gone to pot. After all, how much finesse does it take to chow down a Big Mac, not to mention finger-lickin'-good chicken? As yummy as they may be, these foods have never found a fork they could love. It's no wonder that many aspiring young businesswomen get high marks for ability, but score zero when it comes to executive table manners.

SOB STORIES

There's many a sad story about eager beaver job candidates who made the preliminary cut, and then blew it when they were invited to lunch or dinner by their potential bosses. These young women never realized they were being judged on how savvy they were in the social department. According to the aforementioned Patricia Francy, the treasurer of Columbia University, New York City's third largest employer, "Prospective employers who invite you to dine aren't just trying to make you think they're nice folks. Sure, they want to get to know you better, but their hidden agenda is far more significant. Their real purpose is to scout out how effectively you handle yourself in business/social situations."

Do you have what it takes to entertain a client? Can you properly represent the company at a business dinner? Companies know, and you should too, that table manners reveal far more about you than you might think. Your skills at the table send a message faster than a fax as to whether you're executive-grade material or not.

DINING IN THREE ACTS

ACT I: IN THE BEGINNING ACT

Sit down (straight, no slouching), put your napkin on your lap, and keep your elbows off the table. If you're nervous and need something to do with your hands, take a few sips of water. Just so you don't drink someone else's: *Your* water glass is on the right. It's easy to remember if you say to yourself that drinking water is always the *right* thing to do. Conversely, *your* bread plate is on your left. If you've still got butterflies, you can always butter a bit of bread (*never* the whole piece). Make sure it's on the plate and not in your palm.

You may be worried about which knife and fork to use,

especially if there's a lot of silverware at your place. It's so simple, it's unbelieveable. As the first course is served, just take the utensils that are on the farthest end of your table setting, and work inward with each course. And, of course, you won't start eating until everyone else at the table has been served.

GAUCHE GAFFE: If you discover something yucky in your food, don't make a scene. Let's say there's a fly swimming in your soup. No one says you have to grin and bear it, just stop eating. If you're in someone's home, they'll soon notice that you're not partaking. You can always say something like, "Oh, I believe there's a fly in the ointment," or whatever silly phrase comes to mind. On the other hand, if you're in a restaurant, quietly call the waiter over and point to the intruder.

ACT II: IN THE MIDDLE

Your courtesy coach says never, but never, wave your knife and fork around while you're talking. Use them to eat with, not to gesture. Take your sweet time eating your meal. It's gauche to gobble food down. Try midget bites, not giant ones. Don't get caught reaching across the table for the salt or pepper (the ol' "boardinghouse reach"); ask someone to please pass it to you instead. And your fingers aren't utensils, so don't use them to push food onto your fork. Just use a cracker or a small piece of bread instead. Don't stab the peas, either; just slide them onto your fork. If you have to leave the table during the meal, fold your napkin, place it on the chair, and then push the chair in. Don't leave it on the table; your tablemates won't enjoy looking at a soiled napkin.

GAUCHE GAFFE: Don't chew with your mouth open or talk with your mouth full of food. If you're asked a question in mid-bite, just hold your finger up to politely indicate: "please wait a second."

ACT III: AT THE END

When you've finished eating, put your knife and fork on the right side of the plate, pointing them slightly to the left. You can figure this out if you imagine your plate is a clock, and the knife and fork read twenty minutes after four. This is a universal sign that waiters across the world recognize to mean you're finished. In many countries, if you fail to do this they won't clear your plate, since they'll think you're still eating. Put your napkin next to your plate on the left side. That's usually where it is at the beginning of a meal. Once the plates are removed, leave your napkin there. Don't refold it or ball it up. And never stack your empty plates; that's for the busboy.

GAUCHE GAFFE: After you've finished eating, never smoke without asking if it's okay. At a business function, it's best not to do it at all. Most businesses and homes today are smoke-free, and frown on the habit.

EATING STYLES

When eating, you may properly hold your utensils in one of two ways: either American or European style. Since most people in the United States utilize the former (when in Rome, do as the Romans do), let's talk about the traditional way we eat in our country. American style is to hold the fork in your left hand and the knife in your right hand when cutting the food and then switch the fork to your right hand when putting the food in your mouth. Some people alternate eating styles, especially when they're traveling in Europe. Either way is perfectly proper. Whichever style you choose, just make sure you do it correctly.

Don't be overeager and cut all your food at once, as if you were preparing to feed a small child. Just one or two pieces at a time is about right. When you've finished cutting, place the knife horizontally at the top of your plate, and switch the fork (with the food still on it) to your right hand to begin eating.

GAUCHE GAFFE: If your silverware is dirty, don't make a fuss. If you're at a restaurant, just ask the waiter for a replacement. If you're in someone's home, try to discreetly wipe it off.

SIPPING TIME

When you're eating soup, sip, don't slurp. Why amuse the room? Instead, quietly sip a spoonful at a time. Use the larger, round spoon, not the teaspoon. And don't fill it to the brim, since that gets too sloppy. It's easy to spill it on the table, or down your front when the spoon is too full. Move the spoon away from you, and then raise it to your mouth. Don't ever tilt the bowl toward you to catch the last few drops. Remember, you're not supposed to act like this is the first meal you've had in a week. Last of all, put the spoon on the plate beneath the bowl between sips.

When You're the Host

Go to any upscale restaurant, particularly at lunchtime and, with rare exception, the tables will be jam-packed with businesspeople selling something. The business lunch—or dinner—is an accepted part of executive life. It gives everyone time to have meaningful meetings without the pressure of phone calls and other interruptions.

Business entertaining allows us to "sell" our products—anything from widgets to ourselves—in pleasant surroundings, enhanced by good food and drink. But all this time, effort, and money will be a total waste if you don't know how to host a meal properly. As with everything else in business, there are definite rules to follow when you play host.

Be an Early Bird

Unless you've fallen down the stairs and broken both legs, *always* arrive a few minutes early so that you can be on hand to greet your guest or guests. It's a nice gesture that makes them feel you're glad they could take the time to join you. This will also give you the chance to scout out a "good" table and glance at the menu or wine list so that you'll be able to suggest some of the restaurant's better dishes, another nice touch. All of this not only shows you are a responsible host and puts you more in charge, it makes your guests feel more welcome. That's the way it should be if you want to look professional when you entertain.

"A Bottle of Vino, Please"

If the occasion calls for wine, and your knowledge is nil, don't worry! Just ask the waitperson to suggest an appropriate bottle. If you tell her or him you'd like "good wine and good value," it will be understood that you don't want something that costs more than a month's rent. Never feel that because you're the host, you have to blow a wad on wine. In fact, you'll look more sophisticated if you buy a bottle that tastes good but isn't ridiculously expensive.

If your guest wants a cocktail and you don't, it's never necessary that you have one, too, just to be polite. Instead, order a glass of juice or anything else that's nonalcoholic, to keep her or him company. This way your guest won't feel awkward about drinking if you're not. If you feel uncomfortable about not imbibing with your tablemate, you can always use a line like, "I'm sorry, but I think I'll skip it today," or "I have an important meeting this afternoon."

CHOW TIME

When the food arrives, take a few bites before launching into your sales pitch or a long business discussion. You can't successfully sell anything if your guests are hungry and dying to dig in. Their minds will be more on eating food than on listening to whatever it is you want to talk about.

Don't order messy foods that are difficult to handle, no matter how much you like them. If you're struggling with slippery spaghetti strands or grappling with greasy spareribs, you can't make much of an impression. And forget corn on the cob (it gets stuck in your teeth) and lobster. Foods that can be easily cut and eaten, without a lot of work, are best. Go for fish, sliced meat (no big chunks), bite-sized pasta, or even a vegetable plate. Sawing into a T-bone or dissecting a Cornish game hen takes too much concentration.

When you're led to your table and find that it has two "views"—one facing the people in the restaurant and the other a blank wall (or the kitchen)—the polite host takes the less favorable seat.

If you know your guest is a smoker, and you can bear it, ask your guest if she or he would prefer to sit in the smoking section. However, with all the emphasis on non-smoking these days, no one says you *have* to do this.

CARRY THE BALL

Nothing is worse than taking someone out to lunch or dinner and having an awkward silence descend on the table. This is particularly deadly when you're entertaining a client. I know an account executive for a popular women's magazine who dreads these silences so much that she prepares a "talk sheet." Liz says, "First, I list topics I want to cover for business. Then, I throw in any news items I've just heard that morning in case there's any time left over." This sheet enables Liz to get the conversation going before discussing the business at hand as well as giving her something to discuss after business is over.

GAUCHE GAFFE: Don't use your cell phone at the table, even if it's urgent business. You'll come across as boorish and inconsiderate of other diners, who aren't interested in your latest crisis. Either get up and go to the public telephones, or head for the restroom and use your own.

TIPPING

Tipping is so simple. Why do so many otherwise savvy women get so flustered? First of all, your tip should be based on the bill before tax is added; otherwise, you'll be overtipping. The rule of thumb is to leave at least 15 percent. A quick way a lot of people do the math is to just double the tax, as long as it's around 8 percent. Otherwise, take 10 percent of the bill (which is easy to figure out) and then add half of that amount. In other words, if your bill is $50, take 10 percent (or $5) plus half of that ($2.50). So your total tip is

$7.50. Let's say the service was especially good and the waiter made you look really great to your business associates; you might up the tip to 20 percent, or $10 in the above case.

When you entertain for business, you want everything to go smoothly, with nothing to interrupt the matter at hand. The maitre d' can help you accomplish this by greeting you by name, getting you a good table, and intervening if there's a problem. In that case, fold a $5 bill in half, and put it in his palm—and do it very unobtrusively. Don't announce it, just smile and walk to your table. Most men, who automatically get better service anyway, tip the maitre d' *after* the meal. Unless I'm well known at a restaurant, I usually do it *beforehand* because it guarantees that I'll be well taken care of—which a woman can't always count on. As much as women like to explore and discover new restaurants, it makes more sense for business entertaining to frequent the same restaurant so that they'll begin to recognize you.

WHEN YOU'RE THE GUEST

Being an ideal guest is an art. It's not that complicated but it does take some thought. The rewards can be great—you'll be invited to the best parties, meet exciting new people, and, who knows, you may even get a job out of it.

The rules for "guesting" are pretty much the same for both business and social occasions. If you follow the "Dining in Three Acts" guidelines set forth earlier in this chapter, your basic table manners will be up to par. However, being a superstar guest-meister requires far more than that. You must also know how to extend yourself in a thoughtful and interesting manner. Some people may think it's chic to arrive late, but savvy guests know better—it borders on rudeness unless there's a very good reason. A few minutes is okay but try not to make it more than fifteen. Additionally, a thoughtful guest will always call to let the hostess know she's been delayed.

GAUCHE GAFFE: Waiting to respond to invitations until the last minute is especially impolite. Besides, it makes you look like you're waiting for a "better" offer. Never assume that the host knows you're coming. Those four little letters—RSVP—say it's necessary to take a minute to call and say yes or no. Plus, never bring an uninvited guest to a party, business or social, unless you've asked your host's permission first. Even if it's a stand-up cocktail party, your host may not want extra guests for any number of reasons. If you're found guilty of either one of these social gaffes, the invites will dry up sooner than you can imagine.

Ideal guests make it their business to be accommodating from arrival to departure time. After greeting the host or hostess, they work at being civil and social to everyone who's there. They know it's their job to circulate through the whole room and not ignore anyone. Don't obviously play up to your boss or any other important executive when you're at a party. Never feel free to corral her or him and chatter away. VIPs don't like to be cornered. Plus, it makes them think you don't know how to behave in social situations. Besides, your fellow guests are bound to resent your monopolizing Ms. or Mr. Big; they'd like to say hello, too.

When savvy guests sit down to eat, they realize they have an obligation to divide their time equally between the people seated on both sides of them. If they don't like one of their dinner partners, they still make an attempt to at least be courteous and not make a scene.

GAUCHE GAFFE: Don't dare switch place cards because you've spied someone else you'd rather sit next to. That's considered a big no-no and will label you as an aggressive witch (or another rhyming word!)

Never make a fuss if you're served something you don't like. Just push it around on your plate and pretend you're enjoying it. Most of the time your tablemates won't even notice you're not touching the tomatoes or whatever. In these vegetarian days, many people don't eat meat (including poultry). If you're hosting a dinner in your home, try to offer rice or pasta dishes and plenty of vegetables for the non-meat eaters. On the other hand, if you're the guest and your host happens to notice you passed on the pork roast, for example, it's perfectly all right to say you're a vegetarian. With so much stress on health and nutrition these days, they'll usually understand.

Good guests also observe a couple of other rituals. They're respectful of the dress code. Ignoring it will kill you in business and social circles faster than anything. Grunge is always gauche, and "casual" is, too, if everyone else is wearing her business best. If the host's invitation doesn't tell you whether the party is formal (black tie), business dress, or casual, it's fine to ask! Thoughtful guests also know when to leave. There's nothing worse than having people hang around endlessly when the hostess wants to clean up or go to bed. If this happens to you, just say to the hangers-on, "It was great to see you and let's do this again."

When you're a guest, it's always a nice touch to send a handwritten thank-you note to your host without undue delay. It loses its impact if you wait too long. A phone call is also acceptable, but a bit less elegant. You need to do it immediately, though, preferably the next day.

PRIVATE PLANE PROTOCOL

You may not be eligible for this corporate perk yet, but I'm counting on you to reach that level since you had the good sense to read this book. When you're invited to fly on the company jet, or anyone else's, there are hard and fast rules you must follow. If you don't, you'll be viewed as mannerless and inexperienced. To project an executive image, here's your Wild Blue Yonder laundry list:

1. Don't get to the airport on time, *be early*. It's the height of rudeness to arrive even one minute late and some hosts will leave without you. After all, they're doing you a

favor by inviting you to fly in such luxury. Instead, arrive at least a half hour before departure. This not only shows consideration for your hosts, but gives them the prerogative to leave earlier than the announced takeoff time if they wish.

When I became a corporate vice-president of Colgate-Palmolive, I was invited to ride on the company jet from time to time. On my first trip I made the mistake of getting there only a few minutes before departure. The CEO was very annoyed. He had planned to leave earlier due to a tight meeting schedule in the next city. The flight started off on the wrong foot because I didn't realize that private plane protocol means getting there *really* early. The reason for this is that corporate jets, unlike commercial carriers, are often able to take off earlier than their scheduled departure time.

2. It's rude to bring more than two or three pieces of luggage aboard, and even those shouldn't be too large, particularly if the plane has its full quota of passengers. If you can't squeeze all your belongings into two suitcases (I confess, sometimes I can't), FedEx the rest ahead, as I do. And when I'm a guest on someone else's plane, I always call my host's secretary and ask if it's okay for me to bring on those two pieces of baggage.

3. If you board before anyone else arrives, don't grab any seat, since it could be your host's regular spot. Always ask the crew where you should sit.

4. Even though the plane is private, don't dress as if you're going on a picnic. You want your appearance to be

appropriate for the occasion. Pantssuits (matching pants and jacket) are okay, just no grunge.

5. Don't request special foods; eat what's offered. After all, it's not a flying restaurant!

6. If the plane doesn't have a flight attendant (lots of small jets don't), try to be helpful. Offer to get something to drink for other passengers, or to pass food around—not because you're a woman, but because you're a well-mannered person. Why should your host have to take care of everything?

7. If the plane has a phone and you feel you must make a call, always ask permission before using it. Air-to-ground contact is very expensive. Never stay on too long.

8. Be a pleasant skyrider. Greet everyone, and give other passengers your name if they don't know you. Don't discuss controversial subjects or make off-color remarks.

9. If you use the restroom, be considerate of other passengers. Mop up any water you may have splashed on the sink, and don't leave soiled tissues lying around.

10. When you're a guest on someone else's plane, always arrange your own ground transportation at your destination. Taxis are not plentiful at private airports, and your host may not have provided transportation for you, expecting you to take care of this detail. If you haven't, you'll come across as a moocher, or at least as someone who's not used to the luxury of flying in private aircraft.

11. After you land, it helps to identify your own luggage, especially if everyone is going in different directions. Otherwise yours just might be sent to the wrong place. Always make sure your luggage is tagged, in case this happens.

12. Always thank the captain and crew when you leave, and be sure to send your sky host a note expressing your gratitude.

MANNERS: A TWO-WAY STREET

As the old saying goes, what's sauce for the goose is sauce for the gander. When applied to manners, you have the right to expect, demand, and insist on good ones; you don't have to put up with bad manners from anyone. This definitely includes the people you work with.

If a co-worker starts shouting at you, let him know his behavior is unacceptable. It's never necessary to yell back. Instead, tell him you'd like to discuss the subject later, when it's a "better" time for him, and then walk away. Okay, so you can't do this with your boss, but your body language can tell her that she's out of line. My advice is to look her directly in the eye while she's talking to you, and don't smile. (A smile sends the wrong signal; you're *concerned*, not happy.) Whatever you do, don't cry. Tears are too personal and water down your executive image, to say the least.

If your boss happens to criticize you in front of others, grin and bear it for the moment. Then make an appointment to see her alone and say, "In the future, I'd appreciate it if you'd talk to me privately when you have any criticism about my performance." There's an important rationale behind this: Just as you always want to make your boss look good, she, in turn, should want to do the same for you, as long as you're giving your all.

KILL THEM SWEETLY

When it comes to dealing with people who are rude, you can always try killing them with kindness. Southerners seem to know how to do this better than anyone. Even when someone is rude to them, they're still pleasant. They don't curse or raise their voices, or behave as obnoxiously as the person who has just insulted them. Instead they politely, but firmly, make their point and then drop the subject. I've seen many a raging bull tamed by this technique. Try it!

For example, if a service establishment (some trendy restaurant, let's say), treats you badly, complain to the management quietly, but firmly. If a waiter is rude to you, don't stand for it. But, again, handle it nicely.

Men rarely seem to tolerate poor service in restaurants, as women sometimes do. My husband once took the CEO of a multibillion-dollar conglomerate to lunch. While they were ordering, the waiter started giving them "attitude." He refused to look them in the eye (a bad sign), and he seemed to resent having to answer questions about the menu. Their reaction? They just walked out and found another restaurant. (There's always another one!) As they left, they told the maitre d' what had happened, although everyone around them had already gotten the message.

Sadly, women encounter this kind of tacky treatment frequently and it's not easy to handle. When the situation warrants, however, a woman should take appropriate action without feeling guilty about it. Just be careful how you handle something like this. Don't make a big scene. A woman is under far greater scrutiny than a man in similar situations. Again, be firm but polite. Never yell or over explain. Make your point and end it. They'll get the message fast enough.

The most meaningful way to give a lesson in manners is to withhold your business. Even chichi boutiques have learned the hard way that if they treat customers badly, their bottom line suffers.

WRAP-UP

A successful business executive has many skills. One of the most important is knowing how to treat others. A CEO who's a good friend of mine attributes his great career success to his mother. He says, "She taught me manners at a very early age, and drummed it into me to treat others with respect. My people skills have helped me succeed every bit as much as my business know-how."

Being considerate of others does as much for your image as your business skills do. Kindness usually breeds kindness, just as displaying a lack of manners will only hurt you personally and professionally, in the long run. Being thoughtful

in your dealings with others doesn't mean you have to be a
patsy and give in to everyone, whether you want to or not.
It's simply a matter of living by the Golden Rule: *Do unto
others as you would have them do unto you.*

GETTING YOUR ACT TOGETHER

"I've seen a lot of guys who are smarter than I am and a lot who know more about cars. And yet I've lost them in the smoke. Why? Because I'm tough? No, you've got to know how to talk to them, plain and simple."

These words were written by Lee Iacocca, one of the best-known executives in corporate America, and probably the only one who comes to mind if you're talking about the automotive industry. Why is Iacocca so familiar to everyone? His movie star looks? His brilliance? His great wit? Actually, you know who he is for a very significant reason—he's *always* talking. His down-to-earth speeches have been credited with single-handedly saving Chrysler Corporation from extinction when it ran into severe financial difficulties in the '80s.

Like Lee Iacocca, learn how to communicate in public if you want to be supersuccessful. Am I for real? Absolutely!

In business, you'll be taken more seriously. In private, you'll be admired for a talent that people would *kill* for. Because it's not a skill that the average person works at, good speakers are few and far between. This means not only less competition but an even greater opportunity for *you* to succeed.

The ability to express yourself in front of others automatically positions you as a leader. It says, "Hey, world, what I have to say is worth listening to." Speaking in public is so powerful a weapon that women once were run out of town or even *arrested* for doing it! Thank goodness that's no longer the case, but some women act as if it's still a possibility, and completely shy away from public speaking. That's unfortunate. The ability to communicate clearly often means the difference between success and failure in today's competitive business climate.

YOUR TICKET TO THE TOP

If being able to speak in public can save a billion-dollar auto company and make Lee Iacocca a household name, imagine what it can do for *your* career. For gonnabe execs, public speaking skills can be a ticket to the top. If you want to reach that level, you must be able to convince and inspire people. There's no better way to motivate others than through skillful speaking.

Besides, how many activities do you know that can put you in the spotlight, make you an authority, raise your profile, earn you a promotion, win you new friends, or crown you "Queen for a Day"? When the time comes that you're asked to give a speech, don't panic. You, too, can become a pro through adequate preparation, research, and rehearsal. It may sound oh-so-simple but, believe me, it worked for me and countless others. Guaranteed, it'll work for you, too.

PREPARATION: THE WHO

Preparing for a speech isn't particularly exciting, but it pays off. Begin by grilling the program coordinator or whoever asked you to speak. Find out every pertinent piece of information about your audience that you can. What's important to them? Why are they there? What can you tell them that they haven't heard before?

Is your audience all male, all female, or mixed? How many people are expected to attend? What are their jobs and level of knowledge? Has this specific group ever been addressed by someone with your particular expertise, or will what you have to say be new to them? Is it a "captive" audience, filled with people who have to be there whether they want to or not? (If so, you'll have to work extra hard at keeping their interest.)

Even if you know most of the people you'll be speaking to (maybe they work for the same company you do), update yourself. For example, if you're in advertising and you're going to be addressing the sales group, find out what's happening with them. Are sales going through the roof, or are they lagging behind? Are they introducing a new product or service? What are their goals for the next quarter?, and so on. You'll come across far better if you appear knowledgeable as to what's happening in *their* world. If you don't make any attempt to relate to their problems and/or accomplishments, even company loyalty won't keep them interested in your pearly words.

PREPARATION: THE WHEN

Next, find out exactly *when* you'll be speaking. Before lunch or after? If so, what time? If it's after lunch, keep in mind that most people want to be back at the office by two o'clock. If your speech starts too late, people will start looking at their watches and try to slip out of the room unnoticed. All your hard work will be wasted. Insist that you begin your speech at whatever hour will give you sufficient time not only to deliver it, but to allow for Q&A.

Dinnertime speeches are a whole other hazard. If you've been asked to speak after a long, drawn-out dinner, be aware that people will start to get sleepy and want to go home. And if there's to be a cocktail reception beforehand, plus drinks with dinner, watch out. Your audience may do far worse than just nod off. If there's no other time you can be scheduled to speak, you've got two choices: either keep your speech short— *very* short—or beg off.

Once you've learned about the audience you'll be addressing and when you will speak, you must decide how long you want to talk (if you're given the option), and what presentation style is appropriate for the particular group. Is this an audience that will react better to statistics, graphs, and research analysis? Or is this a group in which a more emotional approach, with personal anecdotes, humor, and opinion, would be better received?

PREPARATION: THE WHERE

Get some information about the setting in which you'll deliver your speech. Is it a large room? Is there a dais? Will there be a podium? Will the audience be at tables or sitting theater-style? On the day of your actual speech, get there as early as you can to psyche out the room. Never—but never—walk into a strange room minutes before you're scheduled to speak. You need time to check out the equipment (microphone, slides, etc.) plus the all-important lighting, which is a subject unto itself. Again, remember that if the lights are too dim, it'll be prime time for your audience to catch a few z's, plus you'll be unable to see your notes.

Don't take *anyone's* word that you have nothing to worry about, that everything will run like clockwork and you needn't bother to check things out beforehand. I've heard that before, only to be confronted with a mike that didn't work, a slide projector that was jammed, or lighting that made the room seem like a deep, dark cave.

RESEARCHING AND WRITING

As my friend Michael Klepper says in his book, *I'd Rather Die Than Give a Speech*, "A speech is more than ideas. It is sound! It is music! It is rhythm! It is rhyme! It is poetry! It is performance!"

But all of that poetry doesn't come easily, and it won't play at all unless it's backed up by research and solid ideas. How do you go about researching a speech? It's as simple as pulling out a piece of paper and writing your topic across the top of the page. Then write down every pertinent idea you can think of. Don't be fussy about this; just list your ideas in no particular order, and don't worry about expressing a complete thought at this stage. Once you've done that, you need to add some meat to the bones and get as much background material as possible. Buy books if necessary, go to the library, get on the Internet, or talk to people with expertise in the field. Any time you can quote from a credible source—a person, a book, a newspaper or magazine, etc.—you lend authority to a speech ("According to acclaimed Hollywood director Steven Spielberg . . ." or "As the *Wall Street Journal* noted recently . . .")

Once you've assembled all your material, experts recommend that you begin your speech by making an outline. This way you'll know exactly which points you want to include. Before you flesh it out, remember you need an obvious beginning, middle and end. These three elements are necessary for a clear and understandable format. The beginning should "grab" the audience's attention, the middle should give the message, and the end should wrap it up. Just remember, writing a speech isn't easy, but it's not rocket science, either.

No matter what your topic is, keep your sentences short! And shorter!! Use action verbs ("sales shot through the roof") instead of passive ones ("sales are up"), and use as many picture words (i.e., imagery) as you can. In other words, describe things so people can "see" what you're saying. Instead of telling them that a snow storm made you late for the meeting, say, "I just left a blizzard that blanketed every inch of town, right up to the tops of the trees." Besides painting a picture, that sentence is effective because of the repetition of the letters *b* and then *t*, a device known as alliteration. It can make your words jump out to your audience.

WRITING WITH STYLE

Before you get started, remind yourself that your primary responsibility is to make it easy for people to understand your presentation from the first word to the last. One way you can do this is by simplifying your language. No thought is so complicated that you can't say it simply, even if you're discussing a technical subject. Use the *KISS technique*—"Keep It Simple, Stupid!"

Remember to be yourself. Feel free to inject your personality into your speech. It's also important to speak the way you always do. If you use words that aren't a normal part of your vocabulary, you'll come off as a phony. To be an effective speaker, you don't have to sound formal or any different from the way you usually do.

Also, make your remarks warm and friendly. One way to do this is to imagine you're talking to a close pal. Every U.S. president has used this technique. FDR had his "fireside chats," George Bush confessed on camera that he hated broccoli; and Bill Clinton either "feels your pain" or tells you about a personal letter he's received from a youngster. In other words, you'll be a better speaker if you talk like a human being, rather than a programmed robot.

Finally, use appropriate quotes whenever you can. They'll make your speech more interesting. For example, when I give a speech about self-confidence, I frequently quote the poet, William Butler Yeats ("I have spread my dreams under your feet/Tread softly because you tread on my dreams"). Your quotes don't always have to be serious, though. You can also refer to a popular song to illustrate a point ("Don't step on my blue suede shoes") or quote a newspaper headline, or refer to something you heard on TV.

GRAB 'EM

At the start of your talk you need a "grabber," something that will get the audience on your side immediately. This is mandatory. If you don't catch their interest within the first minute or two, chances are they won't stay with you. You want your audience not only to *hear* your speech, but to *feel* it.

Many effective speakers, like President John F. Kennedy, "grabbed" their audience by finding a personal mechanism to bond with them. In his famous speech in Berlin, he began by speaking in German—"Ich bin ein Berliner" ("I am a Berliner")—which drove the audience absolutely wild. Other people "grab" attention by focusing on a pertinent piece of local news or making a comment about the particular group they're addressing.

Some people like to open up with a joke. It's great if you

can lighten up your audience and make them smile or laugh. But humor has its hazards, especially if it doesn't come naturally to you. I've heard several speakers try to tell a funny story—only to fall flat on their face, evoking only a few polite titters, or—worse—stony silence. If you're not sure of your ability to tell a joke (and a speech isn't the time to practice)—play it straight. Save the humor for one-on-one meetings or cocktail parties.

DO YOU KNOW THE WAY TO SAN JOSE?

Once you've focused your audience's attention, you've got to let them know where you're going so they can follow. One of the best ways to lead your audience through your speech is by using the old army technique: the Three T's. Tell them what you're going to tell them, tell them, and then tell them again by recapping what you've just told them. Some people say that this technique is old hat and not necessary. Baloney! It's tried and true and provides an easy road map for people to follow.

Finally, make sure your transitions are smooth. Use a bridge as you move from one thought to another. It can be as simple as, "That reminds me of . . ." Or you can use enumeration. For example, "There are three main points I would like to share with you. The first is . . . The second focuses on . . . And, lastly, the third is about . . ." If you don't alert your audience that you're changing lanes, you might confuse them.

Rehearsal

Experts say half of your preparation time should be given to rehearsing your presentation. After you've put your remarks down on paper, sit in a comfortable chair, turn off the phone, and read your speech out loud to yourself. By doing this, you'll discover if you've included words that are difficult for you to pronounce. If so, change them if possible. If not, write them out phonetically. This is also an opportunity to determine if your material is meant for the eye or for the ear. Some phrases are better expressed in written, rather than spoken, form. You'll also find out if your material is repetitive. Be merciless and slash out any extraneous phrases and thoughts.

This is also the right moment to time your speech and make the necessary cuts or additions. It's also the time to decide which words and phrases you want to emphasize. Do one more read-through after you've made your changes to make sure you've covered all your bases. The read-through is not meant to accomplish anything more than allowing you to become completely familiar with your material. This is not the time to "act out" your speech or worry about gestures, body language or vocalization. It's perfectly O.K. to read your speech in a monotone, saving your theatrics for later.

Once More, from the Top

Next, you'll need a full-blown practice session. Either rehearse it in front of a friend or tape record it to see how it sounds. My personal preference is to rehearse in front of at least one other person in order to get their reaction. Your rehearsal audience can tell you if a sentence is too long or convoluted or if what you're saying isn't clear. They'll also be able to give you feedback as to what parts of your speech particularly appeal to them. This is important information that you can build on. For example, if they react positively to certain imagery, you might want to expand it.

I usually rehearse a speech out loud at least ten times. Sometimes I can't stand to go through it again, but I force myself to, anyway. It's boring, time-consuming, and easy to get distracted, but it always pays off. The speech sinks into my brain and I become better able to add the necessary emphasis and gestures that make a speech credible and interesting.

A SPEECH IS MORE THAN JUST WORDS

Experts say the impression you make on an audience depends on more than just your actual speech. It's determined by your *verbal* abilities (what you say), your *vocal* abilities (how you say it), and your *visual* abilities (how you look when you're saying it). Surprisingly, those same experts also suggest that what you say and how you say it accounts for only 45 percent of your appeal. Believe it or not, studies show that the factor that makes the biggest impact on your audience is your visual impression—how you look—which includes the way you dress and how you use your body language. That accounts for 55 percent of the impression you make. This is not to say that you can deliver a lousy speech and get away with it just by looking good. What these studies point out is that there's a lot more to skill on the soapbox than merely opening your mouth.

BODY LINGO IS ALWAYS WORKING

Nonverbal communication is an important part of your visual impact when you're speaking. Body language is a natural reflex, like squinting when the sun is in your eyes, or nodding your head when you agree with someone. We all use it, even when we're not aware of it. The more appropriate your body language is, the more it reinforces your message. Conversely, when it contradicts what you're saying, your whole speech can go down the tube in a nanosecond. To stand stiffly with a weak smile plastered on your face and say, "I'm so happy to be here tonight" turns your audience off right at the start.

You can use your body language effectively during each of the three major phases of delivering a speech—before you speak, while you are speaking, and after you've spoken.

PHASE ONE The first phase starts when you're in the spotlight and about to utter your first word. During those few seconds when the room is perfectly still, people start making judgments about you and your ability to speak. This is the time to capture them with the right body language and to start using your own brand of *ESP*. Here's what to do:

*E*stablish eye contact, scanning left to right.

*S*mile.

*P*ause.

These three things focus your listeners' attention and prepare them to hear your message.

PHASE TWO The second phase when you can use body language to good effect begins when you're actually speaking. To be effective, your body and your words should say the same things at the same time. In order to reinforce your verbal message, lean your body slightly forward. This tells your audience you're reaching out to them—that you want to connect. Conversely, never lean back from the podium. It will make your listeners feel that you're pulling away from the them. Make sure your body motions are fluid, turning and moving easily. Don't keep your hands locked to the podium or by your sides. You'll look stiff and dull.

Use your hands to reinforce your message—but only do what comes naturally. You want your gestures to match the mood of your speech. Don't let your fingers fidget, and be very careful if you wear glasses. It's distracting to gesture with them. Your audience's eyes will follow the glasses instead of what you're saying. Avoid any such D.D.'s—Dangerous Distractions.

THE EYES HAVE IT

Maintain eye contact throughout your speech. Make sure you focus on everyone in the audience. Turn to the left, the middle, and the right side of the room throughout your speech. Don't make anyone feel left out. Find a friendly face to focus on and direct your talk to him or her for a few seconds. This will reinforce your self-confidence and it will show in your face. If you notice a few disinterested faces, take note. You may be losing your audience for one reason or another. If so, pick up your pace and skip any parts of your speech you think they might find boring.

PHASE THREE The third phase in which you should consciously use body language is as soon as you finish speaking. This brief period, while you're still standing at the podium, can be very valuable. Instead of rushing off, stand and use your ESP again:

*E*ye contact! Look directly at your audience for a few seconds.

*S*mile to acknowledge any applause.

*P*ause, nod, and say, "Thank you."

Using your ESP at the end of your talk gives the audience time to absorb your message. Now walk back to your seat at an even, deliberate pace. Not too fast, not too slow, but with your head held high, full of confidence. Body language is an endless subject, but these are the most important parts to re-member when you're speaking.

SETTING THE STAGE

Even seasoned speakers spend some time thinking about how they're going to be introduced before stepping up to the podium. Take it from me, being introduced properly goes a long way toward setting up your speech. The audience needs to know *who* you are and *why* you're qualified to speak on the subject. They'll find it difficult to pay attention to you if they know nothing about your credentials or where you're coming from.

When I was elected the first female vice president in the history of the giant Colgate-Palmolive Company, a lot of or-ganizations were eager to have me address their groups. I once accepted a speaking engagement at a very prestigious meeting of high-level sales executives from around the country. The group requested my bio and assured my office I would be properly introduced. The person introducing me was not only familiar with my background but we had previously worked together.

Guess what he said? "And now I'd like to present Tina Santi Flaherty, who works for Colgate-Palmolive. Tina has some important things to tell us." I was really disappointed. He not only failed to specify what I did at Colgate, but he totally neglected to mention the project we had worked on together, much less the recent promotion I'd gotten, which had made headlines across the country.

By omitting this essential information, he didn't give my speech a proper buildup, which potentially lessened its credibility. After such a ho-hum introduction, why would the audience want to pay special attention to me? How would they know that I had anything meaningful to say? Although it wasn't a total disaster, because I "credentialed" myself when I began talking, we lost the opportunity to whet the audience's appetite. From that time on, whenever I was asked to give a speech, I always sent a suggested introduction (whether requested or not), and brought extra copies to the event in case it was misplaced. Nine times out of ten, the moderator read my intro word for word, just as I had submitted it.

How Will You Be Introduced?

There are several ways to handle your introduction. Preferably, have someone else introduce you—hopefully in glowing and complimentary words that sing your praises. If you want to ensure that your introduction is written in a way you consider appropriate, write your own. It's done all the time. All you have to do beforehand is say to the person who's going to introduce you, "Someone has written an introduction for me that you may want to use." (That someone is *you*, of course, and undoubtedly you'll come up with all sorts of wonderful things to say about yourself.) Just call it "Suggested introduction for [Your Name]."

If it isn't possible to have someone else introduce you, do it yourself. Give your name, title, and a little background that spells out your credentials. It's equally important that your introduction include some personal details about you, such as where you were born. After all, you want people to know you're a warm, fuzzy, adorable person whom they can't resist listening to. Here's an example of an introduction that was given for me when I recently spoke to a large group of university administrators. This is what the program chairman said:

> *To talk to us about what we should—and should not— do to enhance our image is one of the country's most outstanding communications experts—Tina Santi Flaherty.*
>
> *Currently the president of her own marketing and communications company, Image Marketing International, Tina boasts a background that includes corporate vice-presidencies in three of America's largest companies—Grey Advertising, Colgate-Palmolive, and GTE. She was the first and only woman to hold that office in all three corporations.*
>
> *Cited by* Business Week *as one of America's top corporate women, Tina has long been recognized as one of the country's most innovative marketers. She has created numerous campaigns for major corporations that are considered legendary for their imagination and bottom-line effectiveness.*
>
> *In addition to her endeavors as head of her own company, Tina also is renowned for her singular skills as a voluntary fund-raiser for a dozen or so educational organizations that she supports with her head—and her*

heart. She's here to tell us how we can use personal com-
munication skills to improve the image of our university.
   It is my great pleasure to introduce—Tina Santi Flah-
erty!

This introduction was effective because it informed the audience of the following:

• My business background and current position (sets
speech up)

• My industry and media recognition (establishes credibility)

• My overall qualifications to speak on the subject at hand
(essential to hold the audience's attention)

• My philanthropic activities (warm and fuzzy)

AFTER THE BALL IS OVER

Just as the event coordinator owes you a decent introduction, you're due an equally good closing. I once listened to a
pretty interesting speech and when the speaker finished, I was
amazed to hear the chairman say: "Thank you, John. And
now let's break for lunch." Period. John smiled weakly and
darted off the dais.

After all your hard work, a brush-off like this is a double
downer. To help avoid it, ask the event coordinator if she
would like you to prepare a couple of re-cap lines for her to

use following your speech. This is a subtle way of suggesting that your remarks should be acknowledged with more than a mere thank-you, for the audience's sake as well as yours. Just say that you think one or two lines of reference to your topic would be helpful to the audience's understanding of your speech. Something like, "Susan taught us a lot today about XYZ topic. [Then the event coordinator could give one or two examples.] Thank you, Susan, for such an effective presentation."

In other words, all that needs to be done when you've finished speaking is to have the coordinator repeat your topic—briefly—and express proper gratitude for your appearance. That's the least you should expect after all your hard work!

LOOKING THE PART

How should you dress? When you're giving a speech, this isn't the time to wear outlandish clothes, plunging necklines, or denim workshirts. You should wear whatever you would if you were interviewing for a job or meeting with an important client. A well-tailored suit in a neutral shade or muted pattern is always the best choice for a woman, since it conveys authority and a businesslike image.

Navy, gray, brown, or beige suits are always appropriate. Since you don't want to look like "Vampira," it's best to avoid a total black look. It draws the color from your face. One of the most effective speakers I know always tries to wear some shade of red. She says it wakes up her audience. When you're sitting on a dais, a red suit helps you stand out and distinguish yourself from your co-speakers. If you don't have a red one, wear a basic-color suit and a bright blouse, to add zip. Wear small jewelry, nothing that dangles or jangles.

DON'T EVEN THINK ABOUT WEARING...

... an outfit you haven't worn before. Always "test" it out first to make sure it's flattering and fits well. Giving a speech is uncomfortable enough as it is.

... a tight skirt that's so short you have to keep tugging at it to pull it down, especially if you're sitting on a dais. You'll look uncomfortable.

... a loose, fly-away hairdo that you have to keep brushing away from your face or out of your eyes. You'll seem juvenile, and it's distracting.

... sunglasses on stage, unless you want to look like an aging movie star. In fact, unless it's absolutely necessary, don't even wear regular eyeglasses. Contact lenses are a better bet. Glasses can create a barrier between you and your audience.

... stiletto-heeled shoes. Not only are they unbusinesslike, you could break your neck if you have to get on and off a platform.

... extra-heavy make-up. You'll look like a clown, especially if the lights are fluorescent, which casts a harsh glow.

. . . anything you can't resist fiddling with—your beads, buttons, rings. It's distracting.

. . . a slinky, sequined, skintight dress, even if it's an evening event. Save it for a night on the town, *not* for when you're giving a business speech.

Wrap-Up

Now that you know how to get your act together, you're ready for the spotlight. It's time to walk up to the podium and knock 'em dead. The next chapter will tell you how.

SHOWTIME! GIVING A SPEECH

"The ability to speak is a shortcut to distinction. It puts a person in the limelight, raises one head and shoulders above the crowd. And the person who can speak acceptably is usually given credit for an ability out of all proportion to what he or she really possesses."

These words were written by the late Lowell Thomas, the radio and TV newscaster, who was, in his time, one of the best-known, most listened to people in America. He was a major proponent of public speaking. And I agree with him, completely.

The very first speech I gave, at age eleven, before all twenty members of my class, was a big hit. Don't laugh. That positive reception from my fellow fifth-graders was all I needed to get up on my little feet to speak a second time.

In life, one successful experience usually leads to another.

That's certainly been my story, and here I am, some 1,000 speeches later, still doing fine. In fact, I firmly believe that my ability to speak on my feet (which are a bit bigger now!) is primarily responsible for my career success. Not everyone enjoys public speaking, however. According to some surveys, as I'm sure you've heard, the thing people dread most is not death, taxes, or even having a tooth pulled. It's giving a speech!

Everyone gets cold feet before making a speech—from the novice to the most accomplished speaker. After all, who wants to flub up in public? I've heard world-acclaimed speakers deliver their talk and then scurry around to ask a few friends, "Was I okay? Did I do all right?"

Remember, *every* new experience—whether it's learning to swim, drive a car, or, yes, sampling sex—brings its own brand of anxiety the first time around. Why should giving a speech be any different? Once you know what you're doing, it's not half as intimidating as you thought it would be. Although fear may always lurk in the background, *fear* won't be in charge of your speech. *You* will.

TERROR TIME

Fear begins with a deep-down belief that you're going to goof up because you can't do something you're expected to do. And when you're asked to perform an activity—like giving a speech—in front of a group, the panic sets in. You feel that terrible twinge in your stomach, the sudden pounding of your heart, and the urgent need to clear your throat. You wonder how you got into this awful spot and pray that you'll get through it alive.

Is it really possible to overcome the terror of speaking in public? Absolutely, but it won't happen overnight. Unless your fears are caused by deep-seated psychological problems, you can rid yourself of most of them if you're willing to work at it. Although there's no confidence capsule you can swallow to completely cure you of speaker's angst, you can considerably reduce your nervousness. Most professional speakers will tell you that everyone gets stage fright but that it can actually be helpful. This rush of adrenaline not only keeps you alert but ultimately helps you project better.

One way some people have improved their speaking skills is by taking the Dale Carnegie course. This is a very effective method that teaches participants just starting out how to become comfortable speaking in public. According to Ralph Nichols, CEO of the Michigan Dale Carnegie franchise, who has helped train more speakers than anyone alive today, "[t]he Carnegie course utilizes a method that's easy, nonconfrontational, and, in most cases, very successful. Individuals are asked to speak before a small group of their fellow 'students' in short increments which gradually increase until they become comfortable delivering longer talks. I've never seen it fail yet!"

Ralph, whose communications expertise landed him on the cover of *U.S. News & World Report*, knows what he's talking about. People who've taken the Carnegie course swear by it, including the aforementioned Lee Iacocca, who is an enthusiastic graduate. As he told Ralph, that's what made him such a successful speaker. Although the course is very basic, graduates say it's given them the self-confidence they needed to take the edge off their tension. (For the nearest Dale Carnegie course, call 1-800-231-5800, or visit them online at www.dale-carnegie.com.)

Others have joined Toastmasters International, the world's largest communications organization devoted to helping people improve their speaking skills. (To find the nearest Toastmasters group, call 1-800-993-7732.)

MORE OF MY STORY

The fear of rejection, along with the potential of making a fool of oneself, play a big part in most people's fear of public speaking. Some never get past it, but others are able to overcome it. Case in point: After hundreds of successful speaking engagements, I had one terrible experience at a sports banquet that almost did me in. Prior to this, every audience that I had appeared before thought I was terrific. People always went out of their way to tell me how "good" I was and how much my message meant to them. I always left the podium on a "high." This particular group, primarily professional athletes, not only wasn't interested in what I was saying, they were so full of predinner drinks that they started interrupting me. For the first time in my life, I wasn't getting through to my audience. I couldn't believe it was happening to me. I cut my speech short and left the podium. It was a real downer.

AN OLYMPIC TRY

The experience haunted me so that the last thing in the world I wanted to do was give a speech. However, fate intervened. A few weeks later I was unexpectedly asked to make some impromptu remarks at a business dinner. I hesitated but quickly realized it would have been awkward for me to decline. Besides, this was a group I knew was on my side. I couldn't get out of it. As I walked up to the podium, I gave myself a fast pep talk. I reminded myself that I had always been an effective speaker before and that people liked listening to me. At the same time, I visualized myself speaking confidently to the group and having them listen with interest. When I began to talk, my heart started to pound and for a few seconds I felt those same waves of doubt I'd experienced a month earlier. But I refused to give in to it. As I continued to speak, my old self-confidence snapped back and I quickly realized that this group—whom I knew well—was all for me, unlike the previous audience. By the end of the speech, I was more or less my old self.

What did I learn from this? That fear of failure is very real, even to seasoned speakers like myself. It's something you have to not only face, but fight. It's what Olympic figure skaters do when they fall. They get right up and keep on going. My refusal to let that one unfortunate experience undermine my self-confidence allowed me to continue with what is still a successful career in public speaking. You have the same choice. You can let your early defeats paralyze you or you can try again. But make sure you pick your spots carefully, as I did for my "comeback."

My friend John Rosenwald, whom you read about earlier, gives the best advice on this. In his words: "Remember the instructions on a jar of mayonnaise—keep cool, but don't freeze."

Tip

When you're just beginning to speak in public, try to do it in front of a smallish audience that you know will be friendly to you. It obviously makes more sense than starting out with a crowd of strangers who've never heard of you. It's just too intimidating, to say the least!

BREAKING THROUGH

If one bad episode could unnerve an experienced speaker like me, it's easy to imagine how difficult it is for others to break through their fear of performing in public.

There are, however, definite ways to calm your nerves and ultimately win your audience over even if you're shaking in your boots when you get up to speak. Once you have a firm grasp of the basic techniques involved, as outlined in the previous chapter, you'll find it's not that difficult to deliver an effective speech.

WHAT MAKES A SPEAKER GREAT?

Some speakers have built legendary reputations based on their ability to captivate an audience. John F. Kennedy, for one, never failed to mesmerize a crowd. Margaret Thatcher's masterful deliveries during her public career always held an audience in awe. Another British prime minister, Winston Churchill, is considered one of the greatest orators of all time. What did they have that others don't?

What these three share with all great speakers is knowing how to personally connect with their audience. The very best become one with their listeners. This is the single most important factor when speaking. Additionally, their speeches are full of vim and vigor—colorful, yet informative; strong, yet caring. In observing these individuals, as well as other powerful speakers, I've noted that they all have certain traits in common. Here's my take on their tricks of the trade.

Master communicators keep their speeches to an appropriate length. Twenty or twenty-five minutes is about right. There's an old, politically incorrect joke that compares a speech to a woman's skirt—long enough to cover the subject matter, but short enough to keep it interesting. One of the speakers at the 1988 Democratic National Convention apparently didn't know about this rule. You may remember a state governor, little known at the time, whose speech was so long and labored that his audience burst into wild applause when he finally said: "And, in closing . . ." That speaker was Bill Clinton. He appears to have learned from the experience. Great speakers know that it's better to "leave them wanting more," and that longer frequently isn't better. In fact, short is always sweeter.

Master communicators (MCs) also establish immediate rapport with their audience. They make sure they bond with them *verbally* and *visually* in the first couple of sentences. Research suggests that people make up their minds whether or not to like you within one minute after you start.

If you want to connect with your audience, try referring to an event most of your listeners are familiar with. Another way to bond is to work in a local reference—an individual, an "inside" joke, or even a hometown sports team. For example, whenever I speak in Pittsburgh, I always start off by mentioning their wildly popular football team, the Pittsburgh Steelers. (I'm a big Steelers fan.)

Along with verbal bonding, communications experts also use eye contact to capture their audience. In that all-important opening minute, don't imitate an ostrich. Look at your listeners, not your speech. If you bury your head in your notes, you'll lose your audience. People will feel you don't know your subject matter well enough, plus they'll be *bored* looking at the top of your head. To avoid this, always memorize at least the first page.

To effectively use eye contact, picture a metronome swinging from left to right. When you start to talk, look to your left and say a few words—slowly move to the middle and equally slowly look to the right. Then repeat the process in no particular order. If your eye contact doesn't include the whole audience, the people you exclude will tune out.

If you want your speech to have drama and impact, effective body language is essential. Every great speaker takes advantage of it. Two or three simple gestures are plenty. When I recently gave a speech in Dallas, to convey that I loved the city, I crossed my arms over my heart with closed fists—the sign for "love." I deliberately used sign language, as it's a very visual medium, where gestures are larger than life.

Another technique master communicators insist on is proper lighting. You might not know this, but former Texas governor Ann Richards, a down-home master communicator, frequently travels with her own lighting and audio crew. She understands how important lighting and sound are when you're trying to reach an audience. Always check the lighting in advance of your speech. If it seems that you've heard this before, it's because I can't emphasize it enough. If the lights are too dim, not only can't you see your notes, it's hard for people to see *you*. Your speech won't have the same impact, because the mind processes information through both sight and sound.

Audiences quickly lose interest in someone they can't see or hear too well. As a rule of thumb, it's *always* a mistake to speak in a totally darkened room, even if you're using slides. Unfortunately, a pitch-black room makes it too easy for people to doze off, as mentioned earlier.

Master communicators are always *totally familiar with their material* and know it backwards and forwards. This gives their speech authority and credibility. If you're fully familiar with your material, it also frees you from worrying about what you're going to say next. You can even throw in a few ad libs without losing your train of thought.

Some of the greatest speakers of our time memorized their speeches—Winston Churchill, for one—although audiences never knew it. While Churchill appeared to be improvising and speaking without notes, he actually spent hours memorizing his speeches word for word, just as an actor does with a script. I also believe in memorizing the majority of a speech, as opposed to working from an outline. Frequently the lighting, as just mentioned, is so bad you can't see your notes anyway. Besides, if you rehearse your speech enough, you'll practically memorize it.

Churchill used any and every opportunity to rehearse. There's a famous story that one day when he was taking a bath, his valet overhead him speaking loudly and at length. Thinking Churchill was having some kind of trouble, the valet scurried into the bathroom and asked, "Did you call, sir?" "No," Churchill replied. "I was just giving a speech to the House of Commons."

If Churchill had been born a half century later, he'd have had the benefit of a video camera. This can be a speaker's best friend, especially when you're just starting out. Recording yourself is an invaluable aid to getting all the kinks out *before* you go onstage. It will tell you if you're speaking too fast or too slow, if your tone is enthusiastic or monotonous, if you're moving your eyes around or staring straight ahead. It'll also let you know if your sentences are easy to follow or too long and convoluted. And equally important, you'll find out what your body is saying. Are you hunched over or standing tall? Are your hands helping to energize your speech, or are they dangling at your sides like limp fish?

If you can't afford to buy a camcorder, rent or borrow one. It's well worth it!

Master communicators always try to work an unexpected prop into their speech. Find something that graphically illustrates a particular point you want to make. It can work wonders for you. I once coached Teresa Doggett, a first-time political candidate, who asked me how she could make her campaign speech more exciting. I suggested she come up with a prop that symbolized her determination to take on her opponent, despite the overwhelming odds against her.

My idea was for Teresa to buy boxing gloves and paint them bright red so everyone in the audience could see them. As she put them on, she symbolically punched her opponent and boomed out, "I'm going to fight, fight, fight to the finish!" That little touch brought her audience of fourteen thousand people cheering wildly to its feet. Teresa and her boxing gloves made the front page of every newspaper in Texas, as well as receiving spectacular television news coverage. Although Teresa didn't win the election, she made a real name for herself among people who had never heard of her before.

Great speakers realize that proper pacing adds impact to their speech. Certain words should be delivered slowly and deliberately. Numbers, in particular, must be said differently from other words since they're hard to grasp under the best of circumstances. We all know how confusing it sounds when people rattle off numbers too quickly. If your pace is too fast, people will miss what you're saying. Always say numbers slowly, and pause between each set of figures.

Master communicators research their audience beforehand, finding out everything they'll need to know about the group, since their main goal is to reach and motivate them. If they're speaking to a group of Baptist ministers, for example, they'll gear their remarks differently from how they would if they were talking before a political audience. Master communicators can feel the pulse of an audience and know how to play to it. The late, great singer and TV star, Dinah Shore, once taught me a wonderful lesson about how important it is to psyche out your audience. When I told her about the bad experience I'd had with that unruly group who kept talking over my words, she said, "Sister Tina, I would have paused and then said to them, 'Hey, I think you're having more fun than I am, so I'm just going to sit down and join you.' "

If a star as big as Dinah Shore would stop her speech, don't assume that the force of your personality or the significance of your message can overcome an unresponsive group. Sometimes it's impossible to reach your audience—especially if your message and their mood don't mix. As Dinah advised, it's better to acknowledge the temperament of the crowd than to ignore it. As the old saying goes, "If you can't beat 'em, join 'em."

Another rule accomplished speakers follow is to go out of their way to show enthusiasm when they speak. No one enjoys listening to someone who sounds half dead. People much prefer to listen to someone like TV talk-show host Rosie O'Donnell, for example. She walks her voice up and down. It makes you want to hear her every word. If you speak in a monotone, you'll bore your audience even if your words are brilliant.

But don't confuse enthusiasm with gushiness when you speak. Don't let your voice or your words contain too much hero worship or excessive praise. You'll appear far more credible if you speak in a natural, neutral manner. Women have to be especially careful with enthusiasm because their voices normally are higher in pitch than men's. What sounds mesmerizing and dignified in a male voice can seem Betty-Boopish in a woman's. Gushing can even take on sexual connotations if you're speaking about a man.

Master communicators understand that the most powerful speech is one that's clear and direct, with simple words that everyone understands. President Ronald Reagan was called the Great Communicator because he used words that reached everyone, regardless of education or even political affiliation. Great speakers, like President Reagan, realize that the spoken word is far different from the written one. They know that what may be impressive on paper can be hard to understand in a speech. That's why they use short, direct sentences with plenty of action verbs. They also steer away from fancy, foreign phrases or technical terms. Their aim is to make it as easy as possible for their audience to follow what they're saying.

THE TEN MOST COMMON SPEAKING ERRORS

1. Not dressing appropriately

2. Failing to rehearse sufficiently

3. Coming on cold without a proper introduction

4. Burying your head in your notes

5. Not making eye contact with the whole room

6. Making it difficult for your audience to follow you

7. Using fancy words and long, convoluted sentences

8. Talking too fast, especially when citing numbers

9. Lacking enthusiasm and sounding half dead

10. Speaking too long

CALAMITY CONTROL

Through experience, I've accumulated a handful of smaller tips that always help a speaking engagement go more smoothly.

• When you're speaking, always try to use a podium if possible. It's important! Stepping behind one automatically gives you an air of authority, as well as a place to put your notes, a stopwatch, and even a glass of water, a hankie, or whatever. It also gives you something to cling to, especially if you're nervous. In a strange way, it makes you feel protected. The front of the podium is also an ideal place to display the logo of your company or organization. (It's good for photo-ops and serves as a constant reminder to your audience of your affiliation.)

• If you get one of those so-called frogs in your throat, don't try to cough it out. That only irritates the vocal cords when you should be trying to relax them. Either swallow or take a few sips of water to soothe your throat. Before you go on, do what opera singers do to relax their vocal cords— yawn a few times. (In private, of course!)

• Always have a friend or associate bring an extra copy of your speech, just in case. (I once accidentally left mine in the ladies' room, and was there ever a mad scramble till we found it!)

• If your speech runs to more than a couple of pages, don't staple it. Stapled speeches can flop over while you're speaking and cause you to lose your place. It's best to use a three-ring binder, if possible.

• If your speech includes numbers that are significant to your audience, read them slowly. Otherwise they'll be lost. You may also want to put them on paper so they can be handed out after you've spoken.

• If you're planning to give out copies of your speech, *always* wait until *after* you've spoken. If your audience has a copy of the speech in front of them, they'll automatically read it instead of listening to you.

THE Q&A SESSION

The post-speech Q&A session, often pro forma, can also be another opportunity for you to demonstrate your speaking smarts. Reading a prepared speech is one thing. Fielding questions—especially when there's always the chance of a zinger or two—is a horse of a different color.

I've rarely given a speech that hasn't been followed by Q&A. And, to tell you the truth, I enjoy it. It stretches my brain; it tells me what *really* is on the audience's mind (possibly topics I should cover in my next speech); and it allows me to bond even closer with my listeners. Although it is not always a slam dunk, a good Q&A session *can* cover you with even more glory. Just follow these suggestions:

"Plant" a question. Most people are shy about being the first one to speak up. Have an associate in the audience primed to ask a pre-selected question that you can answer off the top of your head. That's not cheating—it's just a way to get things going.

Repeat the question. *Always* repeat the question before you answer it. This gives you a couple of seconds to mentally frame your reply. It's also helpful to people in the back who may not be able to hear questioners who aren't on a mike.

Look directly at the questioner. Pretend he or she is the only person in the room. Even if you think the question is dumb, or way off the subject, treat it respectfully.

Know your topic. Be sure you know your topic from A to Z. Although you've just given a speech on the subject, try to familiarize yourself with fringe areas that might come up in the Q&A sessions.

Don't try to fake it. Never be afraid to say "I don't know the answer to that." It's much better to admit it than to hem and haw and fumble around. Promise the questioner that you'll get the answer for him or her—and be sure you do—even if you have to send it by mail!

Call on other experts. If you have associates with you who are experts in areas that might be the subject of a question, refer it to them. You can just simply say, "I think Marilyn Burns, our director of foreign sales, is the best person to answer that. Marilyn?"

Hear the question out. Always listen to the entire question. Don't interrupt, even if the person seems to be rambling.

Dodge the bullet. If you're asked a question you don't care to answer, do what savvy politicians do: talk around it. You don't *have* to answer a question literally. The same pertains to sensitive questions that are legal or confidential in nature. You have an easy way out—"I'm sorry, but this matter is under litigation, and we're not free to discuss it right now."

THE SPEAKER'S SURVIVAL KIT

How the worm turns! All of a sudden you've graduated from junior speaking status to senior executive rank. You've actually started to get a rep as a snappy speaker whom people enjoy listening to. Organizations start courting you and their invitations asking you to speak begin to arrive. How very flattering! Someone out there actually thinks you have something to say. A program coordinator urges you to check your calendar to see if you're free to give a speech on such-and-such a day. She begs, cajoles and promises it'll be a standing-room-only crowd. She makes you feel like a million bucks, if only you'll say yes. You wonder whether you should accept: After all, this speech isn't something you *have* to do. It's a genuine invitation from someone who thinks you're wonderful. So, ego in hand, you decide to do it. Then what?

Maybe you should stay home and read a good book instead. Why would I—the ever-ready communicator—ever suggest *not* giving a speech? Because I've been burned before. I've bitten like an eager beaver instead of carefully prescreening my invitations. The result? I've spent days—sometimes weeks—preparing a speech only to find myself delivering it to a mere handful of people. The "inviter" overpromised and the "invitee" (me!) fell for it. Conclusion: Not all speaking invitations are worth your while. It takes a lot of time to write, rehearse, and polish a speech that's worth delivering. To prevent you from facing a similar disaster, here's a Speaker's Survival Kit I've devised to save you the pain. Before you say yes to an invitation to speak, do the following:

1. Ask the program coordinator to send you a detailed letter with all the pertinent facts, i.e., when, where, who, and how many are expected to attend.

2. Request a list of previous speakers. Some organizations have the necessary clout to attract top names, others

don't. If you don't recognize a single past speaker, ask your-self if it's worth it.

3. Find out if the organization will help publicize your speech. Ask to see examples of any publicity they set up for previous speakers. You need help in building attendance. Will they schedule an interview for you with the local newspaper? How about TV and radio coverage? Do they have a newsletter they circulate to their members that will highlight your upcoming speech?

4. Find out *exactly* when you'll appear on the program. If you're the next-to-last speaker on the final day of a three-day convention, forget about it. Your audience will be minimal at best. People will be doing last-minute packing or leaving for the airport, not sitting in an auditorium listening to your speech.

The same applies to a speaking slot after dinner. If it's a long, drawn-out affair, especially with an open bar that never closes, think carefully before accepting. No matter how intriguing your speech is, be aware that you're likely to be faced with people who are tipsy, dozing off, or slipping out to get their coats.

5. Ask to see the membership list with titles and company affiliations. Some groups consider this information confidential and won't release it. It's worth a try, even if you only get the names and titles of their officers. It's also helpful to get a profile of the group. It doesn't make sense for you to address

a bunch of people who have absolutely no interest in *your* expertise.

6. If you're asked to speak out of town, be sure to find out who's responsible for travel arrangements and hotel accommodations. If you're with a major corporation, it's generally understood that your company will take care of it. If that's not the case, either you'll have to pay for it out of your own pocket or you should tell the organization that you're not able to speak unless your expenses are covered.

7. Always try to give your speech a catchy title. Even if you're going to be talking about something that's deadly serious—you might even be addressing a funeral directors' convention—one way to assure attendance, unless you're a celebrity, is through your speech's title. It doesn't have to be funny—just catchy. Which title is more engaging: "The Effects of Encroaching Civilization on the Survival of the White Rhinoceros" or "Who Cares about Saving the Nastiest, Meanest Animal on the Planet?" Obviously, the latter is much more provocative.

8. Unless you're a corporate bigshot, it's rare that the organization will pay you a fee for speaking. But, if you think the organization's name will look good on your résumé, do it for free.

As I've told you throughout this book, speaking in public can do wonders for your career, in addition to boosting your self-esteem. But when it's an *elective* activity—not something your boss assigns you—then you've got to pick and choose.

If the circumstances cited above aren't perfect—or nearly so—just say no.

TIME TO TOAST

It's such a happy day! Your brother is marrying the love of his life, who happens to be one of your favorite people. Everyone at the reception is in a great mood, everything has gone without a hitch for the hitching, and now it's time to toast the dearly-weds.

Will you *dare* to be the one who gets up and asks the assemblage to lift their glasses? Probably not. "That's a man's job," some women think. (Says who?) Others feel they wouldn't be any good at it or don't know what to say. I wonder if all this hesitation isn't part of the little-girls-should-be-seen-and-not-heard syndrome.

Why not force yourself to bite the bullet and try giving a toast—at least once? A family celebration is the perfect way to begin. It should be relatively easy for you to handle with people who are so familiar to you. But what if you're in a quasi-business/social situation with lots of strangers present and toasts are being offered? If you want to stand out, just stand up! Hoist your glass and force yourself to say a few words. You don't have to be hilariously funny or over-whelmingly brilliant to give a good toast. It could be as simple as: "I'm Lisa Williams [if some don't know your name] and I want to add my congratulations, too. Here's to Mary for a job well done."

Whatever the occasion, isn't it time that women became as

comfortable as men at making toasts? That they not only *should* do it, but be *expected* to? A heartfelt toast makes everyone feel good and is always welcome, regardless of the gender of the "toaster." Besides, it's a terrific way to get over your fear of speaking in public.

So, let's start with the techniques of toasting. Your first order of duty is to think out what you want to say. If time permits, write it down and say it aloud to yourself a couple of times. Remember to keep it short and be very sincere. Once you're comfortable offering a toast, there may be times you'll want to make an impromptu one. Just make sure it fits the occasion and, again, keep it short and sweet.

Be sure your toast is in good taste. This isn't the time to roast anyone (unless the event is a bona fide "roast") or to try to be ultra funny, unless it comes naturally. If you've had a few drinks and your guard is down, be extra careful you don't offend anyone inadvertently. I recently attended a wedding where the groom's brother—who'd had a few too many—stood up to toast and tried to be humorous. Instead, he wound up hurting the feelings of both the bride and the groom by inappropriately discussing their live-in relationship for the past three years. They were both mortified to have their private life discussed in front of the minister, their parents, and all their friends. It wasn't that the couple was stuffy; it just wasn't the time or the place for that kind of humor.

Toasting needn't be complicated and it's not all that difficult. Plus, it's usually successful if you follow the pointers I've just given you. Think of toasting as an occasion to give someone a compliment in public. Most people love to be at the receiving end of pleasant, "toasty" warm words. Toasting is a great opportunity to "make nice" and to publicly acknowledge someone you think deserves it.

A toast can be dramatic, very simple, or funny. At a farewell party for my executive assistant, Joe, who was leaving to work for another company, I made a few remarks about how much we'd all miss him. Here's what I said:

"Joe did a great job, and it'll be hard to find his equal. Everyone will especially miss his great jokes. I don't want to hurt your feelings, Joe, but I think I've already found your replacement. Let's all stand and raise our glasses to Joe and his successor." The door opened and in shambled an actor I'd hired, dressed in a huge gorilla suit, scratching and making monkey sounds. That happened ten years ago, and people who were there still talk about my toast to Joe.

Now, not every situation lends itself to something as outrageous as my joke on Joe. Your toasts, of course, can always be more conventional. Remember, you don't have to be fabulously funny in order to make an impression. Here are samples of simple toasts you could give at social dinners:

"Let's all raise our glasses to Christina (the woman's name always goes first) and her husband, Brian, on the anniversary of their first date."

"Here's to Maria. She's just written a play that her mother loves. We hope Broadway will, too."

At a business function, it's safer to be more straightforward, unless you have a sense of humor that rivals Jay Leno's.

Here's an example of a toast to give at a business lunch or dinner:

"Here's to our new executive vice-president, Bob Powell. Bill, we wish you luck in your new job, and we'll all be there to help you."

eight

PHONE FINESSE

"I'm a phone fanatic because my business depends on it. Since I'm often out of town or holed up in meetings, I've devised a few tricks to make it easier for people to contact me. Every day I record a different message on my voice mail, giving callers my schedule and exactly when I'll be available. I also tell them that I check my voice mail throughout the day so they'll know their message won't sit around forever. Because people are usually annoyed by voice mail and their inability to reach whomever they're calling, I go out of my way to make my message user-friendly, and even a little personal. For example, when I returned from a business trip to Florida I recorded, 'I'm back from the sunny South, but without a tan because I never left the conference table.' I also give them the name and number of my personal assistant in case they need to speak immediately to a live, warm body."

*T*his *is how* Marina Maher, one of the country's leading communications marketers, handles the phone. Although *she* knows how to make the best use of it, plenty of people don't. They should wise up pronto, because it's estimated we spend as much as 50 percent of our business day on the phone. It's the instrument we use more than all the faxes, computers, and calculators combined. There are fundamental phone techniques that everyone needs to learn if they're going to make maximum use of Alexander Graham Bell's handy little device. Poor telephone habits are a needless risk to your career. They can damage your image as well as nip relationships in the bud before they even get started. Remember, the way you come across on the telephone is a direct extension of yourself. The impression you make on the phone is every bit as important as the one you make in person.

TELEPHONITIS

Most men say that they hate gabbing on the phone and tend to be as brief as possible. Some women, on the other hand, use the telephone more as a social device, losing sight of the fact that it's meant primarily to convey and receive information, and as briefly as possible. Since most business-people have limited time, it's important to know how to use the telephone properly. For example, when you call someone, you should always ask, "Is this a good time for you to talk?" This allows the other party to tell you how much time they've got so you can gear your conversation accordingly. Some callers, however, choose to ignore the fact that you may need to end a conversation, and just keep on talking. I know a metals mogul who says that when he's talking to a rambling mouth, he starts talking slightly faster, and using lots of short words: "Yep," "Nope," "Okay," "Uh-huh." If that doesn't work, he asks, "Can I call you back?" My own telephone conversation-cutter is a simple one. I try to make the other party feel I may be holding *him or her* up, so I say to a gabber, "I better not keep you any longer. Talk to you later." It works every time.

WHAT ARE YOU TALKING ABOUT?

Savvy telephoners know how to cut to the chase. In a face-to-face meeting, you've got time to go into detail, and even throw in a little nonrelated chit-chat. You don't have that luxury on the phone; you have to get to the heart of the matter immediately.

If you want to make sure you're getting your message across, the best way to do it is to write a script. Setting your thoughts down on paper not only ensures that you'll cover all your points, it also will eliminate the hemming and hawing when you can't quite think of what you want to say next. Having it all written down will also give you more confidence, which is bound to show up in your voice.

The aforementioned Marina Maher is a big believer in "scripting." Before she calls someone, she writes down the three most important points she wants to cover. When I asked her, "Why three—why not four or five?" she advised, "Not only do people get tired of listening, they usually can't remember more than three points at one time."

And while you're at it, dig out any relevant material and put it next to your script. It drives me bonkers when people call and start shuffling through papers to find whatever they called to discuss with me. Few things irritate me more.

How Do You Sound?

Your voice is the best ammunition you have when you're on the phone. Try tape recording a few of your own phone calls to improve your telephone technique. When you hear how you sound to others, it enables you to eliminate some of the more common speaking errors, such as repeatedly saying "you know," and "umm." When you listen to the tape, ask yourself:

What's my speed? If you talk too fast—trying to get it all in—you'll give the caller the impression that you're rushing just to get it over with. Too slow, and you can put the person to sleep. The tape will tell you if you should speed up or slow down.

What's my pitch? That same trusty tape can help you decide if your voice range is right. Some women speak in such a high register they'd almost qualify for the opera. A low voice is much more pleasant to the ear, especially on the phone. You can control your pitch, to a degree, simply by thinking before you speak.

How do I "look"? Here's a trick many phone professionals use: they put a mirror on the desk and smile into it before picking up the phone. That smile can actually be "heard" and "seen" by the person you're talking to. It gives your voice, and what you're saying, a terrific lift. Try it!

What's my message? Much as we hate it, we couldn't do without voice mail. But use it properly. Don't leave a long, convoluted message that makes the other person have to re-play it several times to get the gist of it. Keep it to thirty seconds or less. Say your phone and/or fax numbers slowly at the end. It's usually best to repeat them as well.

Who am I? Don't depend on people knowing who you are, either when you answer your own phone or when you're call-ing someone. Always give your full name and, if relevant, your title or department. I've had people phone me "blind," and while the voice was sort of familiar, I couldn't quite pin it down for several seconds. In the meantime, I lost track of what the caller was saying because I was so busy trying to identify who I was talking to.

If someone answers your phone for you, instruct that per-son to get the caller's full name, company affiliation, and tele-phone number, even if the caller says, "She knows me." If you're away from your desk, have your assistant offer some information as to when you'll be back. Be sure you're covered if you're at a late lunch or in the ladies' room. A simple "She's not available now, but I expect her back in x minutes" will do just fine.

MORE PHONE ETIQUETTE

• Try not to let your phone ring more than three times—it gives the impression that nobody's there, that you're not open for business. This is the last thing any company wants a caller to think.

• Never put someone on the speakerphone without asking if it's okay, or at least notifying them. Also remember that the sound only carries for a few feet, so don't wander so far off during the conversation that it's difficult for the caller to hear you. Stay close to the mike!

• Never rely on remembering everything that's been discussed in a business conversation. Take notes and save them.

• "Call Waiting" is great if you only have one line. But when you're the one who made the call, it's very disconcerting to have to tell the person you've phoned: "Oops, I've got another call." When that happens, make sure you tell the second caller that you'll phone back, and get off the line fast. Being put on hold for long minutes is one of the curses of our time.

• Try to answer your own phone whenever possible, instead of acting like a big shot. It's a very impressive gesture.

• Always return phone calls as soon as possible. If you put it off, you give people the impression that their call isn't too important.

• Unless it's an emergency, or you have that kind of understanding, don't call colleagues or clients at home after hours. And even then, make such calls at a reasonable time. Before seven in the morning or after ten at night won't win you any Brownie points.

• Learn to use cell phones at the proper time and place. For example, you'll look like a show-off if you're talking into a telephone while you're walking down the street. And if you use it at a restaurant table, you'll certainly irritate the other diners with your lack of consideration. They're there to have their own conversations and not be forced to be a part of yours. Also remember *when* to turn your cell phone off. I recently forgot, and my phone started ringing in church! Much to my embarrassment, the usher practically pushed me out the door so other people wouldn't be disturbed. You can be sure when I went to a funeral the following week, I turned the power button off.

Wrap-Up

All of these telephone techniques are fairly basic, but as the old Amish saying goes, "Perfection is made up of many trifles, but perfection is no trifle." That's my way of telling you that fundamental phone manners will get you a lot further in life than not having any at all. Because speaking on the phone is so automatic, we often do it without thinking. If you want an edge, give some thought to every call you make. Now's the time to pick up the phone, smile into it, and conquer the world!

nine*nine*

HOW TO MAKE A FOOL
OF YOURSELF IN PUBLIC

Who's kidding whom? Do you really need to take lessons in how to be stupid? While the whole purpose of this book is to clue you in on certain behavior that will make it easier to achieve your goals, frequently it's our *mistakes* that teach us the most. Goofing up may be painful, but it usually enlightens, and hopefully we won't do the same dumb thing twice. Better yet is to learn from *others'* mistakes. Here are a few examples of people who, although they should have known better, somehow managed to make first-class clowns of themselves.

UNDER THE TABLE

First, a tawdry tale of people in high places overestimating their power and pushing the envelope too far. Laurie, an attractive marketing executive from Texas, was attending a charity board meeting and proceeded to take an empty seat at the conference table between two high-powered CEOs.

Halfway into the meeting, she felt a hand on her right knee. Startled, she couldn't believe that this corporate chieftain would be so gross as to try to feel her up. Before she could blast him or punch him in the ribs, Mr. Big on her left grabbed her other knee. Yikes! Double trouble! What to do? Without hesitating, she quickly joined their two hands together under the table, all the while looking at her notes, never making eye contact with her two tormenters. What a brilliant solution to a sticky problem! The Big Boys were left "holding the bag," but obviously not the one they wanted.

LEARNING LESSON: Some high-fliers are so cocky they think they can get away with anything. They can't. Sooner or later they'll get caught. In the meantime, if you're the object of such outrageous behavior, think it through carefully. When you're dealing with people who have more power than you, it calls for real strategic thinking. Laurie's diplomatic handling of this situation was sensible—no big scene, just quietly putting the perps in their place. You can be sure those uncouth codgers treated her with the greatest respect after the failed grope incident.

A JOKE THAT BOMBED

Another area where I've seen friends look like bumble-brains is when they use off-color humor at the wrong time and place with the wrong people. Even some self-proclaimed sophisticates are offended by dirty jokes or use of the *F* word and have a low opinion of anyone who indulges in them. Here's a story about humor that went over like a lead balloon. A very successful couple, whom I happen to know well, wanted to give a birthday party for their good friend "Sharon," in their glorious apartment overlooking New York's Central Park. They told her to invite anyone she liked—business friends, college chums, married pals, etc. They assured her, "It doesn't matter whether we know them or not, Sharon. Any friend of yours is a friend of ours." Sharon, who has a fabulous sense of humor, was extremely popular with people of all kinds—some kooky, others conservative, and a few somewhere in between, like the couple ("Theresa" and "Bob") who were giving the party.

Thirty of Sharon's friends, many of whom the hosts had never met before, showed up to celebrate her thirty-second birthday. Quite a few lived in New York City, but lots drove in from the 'burbs. For cake-cutting time, the couple had ordered a very special dessert that they thought would crack up Sharon and her friends: an exotic creation by the Erotic Baker, specialists in designing cakes with unique frosted sculptures. The one Theresa and Bob chose featured a pink penis on top of a chocolate cake with the inscription, "Keep it up, Sharon!" The party-givers, chuckling to themselves in the kitchen, lit the birthday candles, then brought their masterpiece out to the crowd as they sang, "Happy Birthday, Sharon!" Suddenly there was dead silence in the room. The stiffs from the suburbs, who were in the majority, took one look at the cake and gasped in horror. The rest of the guests, many of whom *did* think it was funny, were too intimidated to laugh. The hosts, who originally thought their idea would provide a big giggle, were mortified. Talk about not reading your audience! This poor couple was so embarrassed they wanted to run away and hide.

LEARNING LESSON: Whether the occasion is business or social, be sure you know your audience before you tell or play a joke. Humor can bomb if you're not certain where people are coming from. What's funny to you may be offensive to someone else.

GETTING TO THE BOTTOM

The cake catastrophe was a planned event, but you never know what *unexpected* thing can happen to make you look foolish. For instance, here's a tale about pantyhose providing an impromptu "plus." Cathy Cash-Spellman, now a bestselling author, kicked off her business career at an advertising agency. One day she was asked to help make a presentation to new clients about future trends in product development. Cathy, who was in her early twenties, had a favorite outfit she always wore when she wanted to make a big impression: a flippy, black miniskirt with a blouse to match. Thinking she looked quite irresistible, she walked up on stage, and prepared to tell the audience how *lemon-scented anything* was the new trend in cleaning products.

Before she could open her mouth, she noticed the audience was smirking and tittering. She had barely started to speak when someone came up on stage, tapped her on the shoulder, and whispered in her ear that there was a slight problem. Apparently, when Cathy went to the ladies' room beforehand to "powder her nose," she'd accidentally caught the back of her skirt in her pantyhose. Unbeknownst to Cathy, she was giving the audience not only a view of the future, but a glimpse of her past that they never expected. Because she has a great sense of humor, she quickly recovered and told the group that "exposing" a product difference is what good advertising is all about!

LEARNING LESSON: If something embarrassing happens, try to make the best of it. Because Cathy made fun of herself, the audience was totally disarmed, instead of feeling sorry for her. Had she gotten all hot and bothered, everyone would have felt ill at ease and her presentation would have been a big bust.

CORPORATE CONFUSION

Sometimes goof-ups happen because we don't have the necessary experience or we just don't think things through adequately. I'll never forget the day when the CEO came into my office shortly after I had joined Colgate-Palmolive. He obviously wanted to speak to me—and he was in a hurry! I was on the phone with a *Wall Street Journal* reporter, who was important to Colgate, and I didn't want to cut him off abruptly. On the other hand, I knew I had to find out immediately what the CEO wanted. I felt like I was caught in the middle. I was fairly new to corporate life and didn't know how to handle such situations. So I chose to continue speaking with the reporter, thinking I could wrap it up in a hurry. Bad choice! The CEO stood there staring at me and finally turned on his heel and left. Later I realized that all I'd had to do was tell the caller that my boss had just walked in and I'd get back to him shortly.

The point of this story is that I probably looked bad to my CEO. I should have been smart enough to know his time was far more limited than mine and that he must have wanted to discuss something really important with me. He rarely, if ever, came to a staffer's office; usually we were summoned to *his*. It didn't take me long to realize that if it ever happened again, I'd be savvy enough to end my phone conversation immediately by saying, "Sorry, I'll have to call you back," no matter who was on the other end of the line.

LEARNING LESSON: Get your priorities straight! My corporate destiny—the rest of my business life—was in the hands of the CEO, not whomever I was speaking to on the phone. Had I explained to the reporter that the CEO had just walked in, he probably would have understood. Undoubtedly he'd have done the same thing had *his* big boss appeared at his desk.

JUST SAY NO

Here's another example of foolish business behavior that almost got someone fired. I needed some information and asked a staff member, "Brad," a simple question about budget projections. Since it was his area of expertise, he was supposed to know the answer. He didn't, so he decided to fudge it. Assuming his figures were accurate, I proceeded to put them in a company memo. Fortunately, before it went out I discovered Brad's error, but from then on he was dead meat in my book. He'd made a fool of himself, but he almost made one of me as well. It's not *nice* to fool Mother Nature—but it's *stupid* to try to do it to your boss!

LEARNING LESSON: Never give a halfway answer, and don't be afraid to say you don't know something. Get all the facts right, or say so if you don't have them. If you acquire the reputation of being a know-it-all when you really aren't, people will begin to distrust everything you say. Eventually you'll be frozen out of the loop.

WHO'S NUMBER ONE?

Another classic case of fools rushing in involved silly sexism at its costliest. The high-profile president of a large public relations agency was pushing hard for the Colgate-Palmolive account. "Fritz" directed 95 percent of his pitch to the male executives in the room, totally ignoring me in the process. Although I wasn't the senior person there, I was the one who would be responsible for supervising the agency because of my communications know-how. I was really bothered by his insulting attitude, and hoped my boss, "Bill," would realize what a jerk Fritz was.

The closing kicker was when Fritz condescendingly said, "Now, Tina, we'll keep you up to date from time to time, but we'll deal directly with Bill." When we left the meeting, Bill, a true feminist, was livid. "If Fritz was stupid enough to put you down in front of others, how is he supposed to handle our public relations?" he asked. "Ninety percent of our customers are women, and he doesn't know how to talk to *one* of them?!" Needless to say, Fritz didn't get our account—just the shaft.

LEARNING LESSON: Before you go to a meeting, always find out who the players are and who's responsible for what. Never assume because someone is young, quiet, or—horrors!—female that she or he is not the leader of the band.

HOLD YOUR TONGUE

Here's another example of the trouble you can get into by not knowing whom you're talking to. I was invited to a very select social/business dinner with top-level bigwigs and their wives in attendance. Spouses were seated at separate tables, next to guests whom the hosts thought were appropriate matches. One of the attendees, "Doug," was a very successful man who had a legendary business reputation. The only problem was that Doug and his wife, "Mallory," were silly snobs who always complained loudly if they weren't seated at the *best* table, next to the most *important* people. After the dinner, Mallory, an acquaintance of mine, came over to me and started complaining about where the host and hostess had seated her husband. "He was at the worst table, with the dullest people possible. He's had it with this crowd and he's not coming back." I looked at Mallory with the biggest smile I could muster, and said, "He happened to be sitting next to me! I'm awfully sorry he didn't enjoy my company." For once in her life Mallory was totally speechless, and she quickly scooted away.

LEARNING LESSON: Be careful before you complain about anyone or anything. You not only should get your facts straight, but also be aware of any connection the person you're complaining to may have with the object of your gripe. You never know whom you may be offending. Also, sit on your big, fat ego! Acting hoity-toity, particularly among your peers, makes you a laughing-stock. Besides, people will gleefully wait for you to get your come-uppance.

BELLY UP TO THE BAR AND BOW OUT

And, of course, the stories about overdoing cocktails are legion and, regrettably, predictable. Regardless of their job level, "too much to drink" has gotten more people in deep trouble than practically anything. "Celine," the executive vice-president of a large consumer products company, was terrified of speaking in public and did everything she could to avoid it. This time it was impossible, since she was going to be honored at an industry dinner and had to accept the award in person. Although Celine was notorious for not being able to handle her liquor, she nonetheless decided to have a few pops before dinner to "calm her nerves."

You guessed it! She not only calmed down, she made a first-class fool of herself in the process. After flubbing her remarks, she almost dropped the award on the floor, before stumbling off the dais. Surrounded by an audience of her peers, Celine's reputation for being a boozer escalated even higher. Soon after, she "decided to leave" the company and start her own business. This story, however, has a happy ending: she went to AA, met and married a man who was a recovering alcoholic, and hasn't had a drink in twenty years. And her business is thriving as well.

LEARNING LESSON: Take it easy—*very* easy—with drinking at company functions. Many a promotion has been postponed and, worse, people have been fired because they got loaded at business do's. And that's especially true for the company's holiday party, where many employees feel anything goes. Wrong! Holiday or not, a business party is a *company* function and the bosses are watching. No matter what the occasion, forget about taking a drink to "loosen up." It's better to be a stiff than a drunk.

KEEP A LID ON IT

Even the ladies' room can get you in trouble. Here's Samantha's story: "My girlfriend and I went to a restaurant in Greenwich Village. We were 'on the town' for a night, without our husbands. As we both sat down to eat, we spotted

Brooke Shields at a table nearby. Naturally, we looked her over and then proceeded to dissect one of the world's most beautiful women. That we were slightly envious of her is an understatement.

"When my friend and I went to the ladies' room, we continued our conversation about Brooke. My first comment was, 'She doesn't look that great.' My friend's reply was, 'You're right, she's looking older and a bit puffy. I bet she couldn't fit into those Calvin Klein jeans now!' At that moment the stall door opened and out came . . . Brooke Shields! She smiled and said, 'Gotcha! You're busted!' My friend stared down at the floor and I started telling Brooke how terribly sorry we were, et cetera, et cetera. She just looked me straight in the eye, gave me a big smile, and walked out the door."

Way to go, Brooke, you've got style!

LEARNING LESSON: Be discreet in public places. Whether you're in the ladies' room or an elevator, at a restaurant or a cocktail party, you never know who may overhear your conversation.

BITE YOUR TONGUE

Even higher-ups are sometimes guilty of indiscretion, often because they're so sure of their position that they feel they can say whatever they want to. If you're the object of someone's uncalled-for criticism, you sometimes have to bite your tongue. Witness Nancy's story: "I was having my final interview, trying for a job at the New York headquarters of an internationally famous art gallery. I was in my late twenties at the time, and dressed to the nines, so I thought I looked pretty good. I walked into the office of the gallery's president and sat next to his desk. He looked me up and down and his first words were, 'Young lady, I don't think you understand what this place is all about. This isn't a chichi job; we require real expertise, not glamour. I think you're the kind of woman who's looking for a husband, not a career.'

"Before I could answer, he got a phone call. I was relieved, because it gave me a chance to collect my thoughts. Although his remarks totally angered me, I knew it wasn't in my best interest to show it. When he got off the phone I said, 'Mr. Burke, we've never met before, so I don't think you should make assumptions about me. Why don't you check with my colleagues to see what my priorities are?' He was stunned for a moment and said, 'I'll just do that. Thank you, that will be all!' Guess what? Despite the fact that he had 'judged the book by its cover,' I was offered the job and accepted it with pleasure! Even though I enjoyed working there, I still thought Burke was a jerk. At least he had the good sense to hire me."

LEARNING LESSON: Mr. Big should have known better than to voice negative, snap judgments about someone whose fate was in his hands. And if you're the subject of such off-the-wall thinking, don't lose your cool under fire. Some people have no finesse and will make offensive remarks. It's especially true that people will say things to a woman, that they wouldn't dream of saying to a man. When you *know* you're in the right, say so, politely, but firmly.

DUMB, DUMBER, AND DUMBEST!

There are a hundred and one ways you can make a fool of yourself; it's much easier than you think. One of the most common is making an ethnic slur. In these days of political correctness, you can easily offend people if you fall back on stereotypical statements. Some things that were considered funny twenty years ago just won't fly today. Race, religion, politics, and sex are areas where you should be extra careful. There's no excuse for anti-female jokes, gay put-downs, anti-Semitic remarks, knocking someone's politics, Catholic-bashing, Polish jokes, or any other distasteful or mean-spirited comments. They're hurtful and you'll not only look foolish if you're guilty of such behavior, you can easily get yourself in trouble on the job.

RÉSUMÉ REJECTS

Résumé bloopers are another costly way to make a fool of yourself. Although the interviewer gets a good chuckle over them, bumbling job applicants get the boot. Not only should *you* spell-check your résumé, but have a few (*smart*) friends look it over, so that it's letter-perfect. Here are the best of the bloopers I've come across:

"Computer *illiterate*." (*No kidding!*)

"I'm entirely *through* in my work; no detail gets by me." (*Maybe one.*)

"Job objective: A position in *pubic* relations." (*Sounds sexy!*)

"Planned and *held up* numerous meetings." (*Better than busting a bank.*)

"I am very dependable. A fast *leaner*." (*Very exotic posture.*)

VERBAL VOIDS

Another way to make yourself look foolish is to feel compelled to fill in the silences when you're at a meeting. It's as important to know when to be quiet as it is to know when to talk. When you spout half-thought-out ideas, you can easily trip yourself up. Take Mark Twain's advice: "It's better to be silent and thought a fool than to speak out and remove all doubt."

Another surefire way to set yourself up for a fall is to justify your actions by saying "I assumed . . ." I once made the mistake of telling the boss from hell, who happened to be in a bad mood, "I assumed the report was okay because . . ." It gave him the perfect opportunity to squash me like a bug and reply, "There's no room for guesswork in business. You either know the facts or you don't. Never *assume* anything if you want to keep working for me." Yes, he was acting like a beast, but somehow using the A word brings out the worst in some people, especially if they're out to get you. Now I always say, "It's my sense that . . ." or "In my opinion . . ." These sound more authoritative and not as if I'm faking it.

Just like the A word, there are certain other phrases you should *never* say to your boss or anyone else in authority. Here are a few:

"It can't be done in that time frame."
(*Well, how long* will *it take?*)

"That's not my problem."
(*Whose is it then?*)

"I'm busy with something else."
(*Not if you work for me, you aren't.*)

"It's probably a dumb idea, but . . ."
(*You've killed your idea before you've started.*)

"You don't understand."
(*Give me the facts and maybe I will.*)

"I'd rather do it *my* way."
(*Forget about your way, just say why you think it should be done differently.*)

"Sorry, but you're wrong."
(*You're asking for trouble.*)

"That's not part of my job."

(*So what? Just do it. Maybe you're being tested to see if you can handle other responsibilities.*)

"We've got a problem. What do you want to do about it?"

(*You're paid to be a problem-solver, not a problem-dumper.*)

VERBAL VICTORIES

Conversely, certain "magic" words are practically guaranteed to please. Unlike the former phrases, they convey enthusiasm and your eagerness to tackle the task at hand.

"I'll work nights or weekends—whatever it takes to get the job done."

"That's really a great idea . . ."

"I understand your concern. What can I do to help?"

"Would you like me to work on this now and hold off on the other project?"

"I'll have it on your desk in two hours."

"There's a problem, but I have several solutions that could work."

"Do I have to get a special pass to come in this weekend? I'd like to finish this project as soon as possible."

WRAP-UP

While looking foolish is something we all want to avoid, sometimes it can't be helped. When you do goof up, don't beat yourself up unmercifully. It's not the end of the world. Chalk it up to experience and learn from it. You can be sure the "dirty cake" couple was careful about using off-color humor again. Just as you can bet that Cathy Cash-Spellman made sure her pantyhose weren't caught in her skirt a second time. Making a fool of yourself every now and then is understandable. But if you don't learn from your mistakes, you'll be a fool forever.

THE LAST ROUND-UP

In the morning, when you're heading off to the job and you want to make it a Big Day—just glance at this and try to remember these points:

THE BIG PICTURE

• You must be fired up with *enthusiasm*, or *you* will be fired.

• The way you *look* is the first thing people notice.

• The way you *act* with colleagues, as well as your boss, is all-important.

• The way you *speak* says as much as the words you use.

• Positive body language will work wonders for your career.

• You can learn to read other people's body language correctly.

PACKAGING YOURSELF

• Dress to fit your company's culture, especially to match the higher-ups.

• Always be ready for an unexpected meeting, even on "casual Fridays."

• Accessories make or break an outfit; keep yours small and tasteful.

• Cleanliness is *always* next to godliness.

• Staying in shape helps you move up the ladder.

• Smile sincerely and as often as warranted.

MAX-ING YOUR MEETINGS

• Pretend every meeting is a job interview and you're being judged.

• Review the meeting materials one more time; don't try to wing it.

• Wear your "executive image," wardrobe and facial expressions.

• Always show up on time.

• Speak up, even if it's just to agree with others' ideas.

; a pertinent prop to make your point mem-

...ys rehearse before presenting, even if you know the subject thoroughly.

• Be attentive; let your body language say that you're listening.

WORKING A ROOM

• Psyche yourself up first.

• Have an "event objective"—Know what you'd like to accomplish.

• Don't wait for people to come up to you; introduce yourself.

• Don't spend the entire time with people you already know.

• Don't be afraid to say hello to bigwigs, but don't hog their time.

• Be all ears when someone's talking to you, even if you're bored.

• Gracefully end pointless conversations so you can circulate.

TALK LIKE A MAN, THINK LIKE A WOMAN

- Don't beat around the bush; speak directly, as men do.

- "Overspeak"—taking too long to get to the point—and wishy-washy expressions don't belong in business.

- Stop apologizing for things that aren't your fault.

- Don't feel obliged to fill in the silence during meetings.

- Don't gush when you're making a simple statement.

- Avoid bloodbaths when you think someone is wrong.

- Forget your sense of entitlement; you have to earn it.

- When the situation warrants, don't be afraid to go it alone.

- Expect to compromise and sacrifice if you want to succeed.

SOCIALIZING FOR SUCCESS

- Everyone agrees, manners are back.

- Etiquette goes far beyond knowing which fork to use.

- It doesn't cost anything to say "please" and "thank-you."

- Make sure your clothes conform to the event; sloppy is out.

• Always have your business cards handy.

• Don't stand for bad service in a restaurant—alert the management.

• Be considerate of others; kindness begets kindness.

GETTING YOUR ACT TOGETHER

• Learn to communicate effectively if you want to rise to the top.

• Don't dodge offers to speak publicly.

• Start with small, intimate, friendly groups.

• Learn all you can about your audience.

• If possible, avoid after-dinner speeches when people may be drowsy.

• Never walk into a room cold; look it over beforehand.

• When writing your speech, use the KISS method (Keep It Simple, Stupid).

• Before you give a speech, Practice, Practice, Practice!

• Be wardrobe wise—no shoddy outfits, no plunging necklines, just business best.

• Use effective body language and maintain constant eye contact.

• Write your own introduction, plus a post-speech send-off, if you want to control your message.

GIVING A SPEECH

• Invest in a Dale Carnegie or Toastmasters course to improve your speaking skills.

• Unless told otherwise, keep your speech to under thirty minutes.

• Practice public speaking by starting with small groups, preferably friends.

• Always rehearse in front of a mirror or with someone who'll give you feedback.

• Find an opening line to establish immediate rapport with your audience.

• Make eye contact with all sides of the room—right, left, and center.

• Connect by memorizing at least the first few pages of your speech.

• If there's Q&A, don't hesitate to admit it if you don't know an answer.

Phone Finesse

• If you smile when you're talking on the phone, you'll sound more pleasant.

• Write a script so you'll say exactly what you called about.

• Keep business conversations as short as possible.

• Always ask whomever you're calling if they have time to talk.

• When leaving a message, say your phone and fax numbers slowly.

• Minimize using a cell phone in public.

CONCLUSION

The preceding pages have explained in detail how to use to your best advantage the various communications channels—verbal skills, appearance, body language, and appropriate business behavior.

In business, as in life, it pays to think it through before you say or do almost anything. "Winging it" won't work, especially in the office. Get into the habit of acting, not *re*acting. Yes, it does mean you can't always be as spontaneous as you'd like, but business is a mental game and it's how you play the game that counts. Like playing chess, every move you make sets you up for a countermove. If your goal is to win, your mind must be concentrated and committed. That's why in a crisis winners *focus*, and losers *freeze*.

If you read this book through carefully, you'll find it much easier to land in the first category—to be a winner. If you stay focused and keep working at it, you'll learn how to maximize your interpersonal skills, which is what good communication is all about. Learning how to communicate effectively is a lifelong process. You may not handle it 100 percent right all the time, but believe me, one day you will. Sometimes life has its ups and downs, and at other times the sun shines through. To keep your optimism ever fertile, read these wise words (on page 176) written a few years ago by the poet Sheenagh Pugh.

SOMETIMES

Sometimes things don't go, after all,
from bad to worse. Some years
muscatel faces down frost; green
thrives; the crops don't fail, sometimes
a man aims high, and all goes well.

A people sometimes will step back from
war; elect an honest man; decide they
care enough, that they can't leave some
stranger poor. Some men become what
they were born for.

Sometimes our best efforts do not go
amiss; sometimes we do as we meant to.
The sun will sometimes melt a field of
sorrow that seemed hard frozen: may it
happen for you.

INDEX